TAKE CHARGE OF YOUR FUTURE

T0352198

By the same author

How to be a People Person

Uniform with this book

TAKE CHARGE OF YOUR FUTURE

BANISH YOUR PAST

Márianna Csóti

Author of *How to be a People Person*

RIGHT WAY

Typeset in 11pt by Letterpart Ltd., Reigate, Surrey.

Printed and bound in Great Britain by Cox & Wyman Ltd., Reading, Berkshire.

The *Right Way* series is published by Elliot Right Way Books, Brighton Road, Lower Kingswood, Tadworth, Surrey, KT20 6TD, U.K. For information about our company and the other books we publish, visit our website at www.right-way.co.uk

For my friends and family

I should like to thank Dr Gill Salmon, Consultant Child and Adolescent Psychiatrist, for her invaluable help with this book; it is much appreciated. Any errors that may remain are down to me!

See my website for a comprehensive list of links to organisations that offer help with a wide variety of difficulties:
www.mariannacsoti.co.uk

Take Charge of Your Future is full of sound practical advice and suggested coping strategies. It will be an invaluable resource for anyone who has wondered about getting professional help for their emotional difficulties. It is written in a clear, accessible and down-to-earth style which will prove popular. General Practitioners would do well to recommend this book to patients who present asking for help either as a stand-alone self-help guide or in conjunction with referral for more 'specialist support'.

Dr Gill Salmon, Consultant Child and Adolescent Psychiatrist

Take Charge of Your Future is to be welcomed in the ever-expanding number of self-help books. It is refreshing to read a book written in everyday language, and which will certainly help many people who want to understand why they feel and act the way they do. This book will take the reader on a voyage of self-discovery and will provide the knowledge to enable anyone to shape their adult self into who they want to be.

Jill Curtis, Psychoanalytic Psychotherapist and Member of the British Association of Psychotherapists

CONTENTS

INTRODUCTION

This book will help you to make enduring personal changes to enhance your life, providing the skills, knowledge and awareness necessary to make it happen. If you feel that you haven't always taken the opportunities that have come your way or that life has sometimes dealt you an unkind hand in the past, this book will help you to take control of your life. It will help you to increase your self-esteem and reach your full potential – becoming the person you were always meant to be.

Part One

Becoming the Adult You Should Be

Each of us is meant to have a character all our own, to be what no other can exactly be, and do what no other can exactly do.
William Ellery Channing (1780–1842)

Part One gives you the skills to shape yourself into the person you really want to, and should, be: it will help you take control of your life to assist you in living the life you deserve.

1

WHO ARE YOU AND WHO SHOULD YOU BE?

Man's main task in life is to give birth to himself, to become what he potentially is.
Erich Fromm (1900–80)

Are you defined by where you are from, where you live, what your personality is like or by whom you mix with? By the job you have or don't have? By how many children you have had or haven't had? By the fact that you are married or single? By the way you think other people view you or have told you they view you? Perhaps what you look like is most important?

All of these things help to define who we are but, even then, it is not the whole picture. Our lives are far more complex: even prioritising these questions gives more insight into who we are.

Lillian felt she was defined by her appearance. She was born with a strawberry birthmark over her right cheek and eye, and felt that whenever she went out without her heavy prescription make-up, people saw only the blemish and not her. Lacking the confidence to be seen at work without her make-up, Lillian felt she was living a lie, pretending to be someone she was not and felt that no one truly knew her. So concerned and self-conscious about her appearance, Lillian could not fully relax when with other people and concentrated her efforts on hiding her face. The rest of her 'self' was ignored, other needs overshadowed by the need to look how other people expected her to look and in fear of not being accepted as she really was.

There can be many reasons why we concentrate on one small part of ourselves at the expense of the rest of us but to continue ignoring the bigger part of ourselves is denying ourselves the right to be us. Throughout life, we develop as people and, if we get it right, we become more and more like ourselves – who we are meant to be. With many of us, what stops us from achieving our full potential is ourselves – in response to unhappy past experiences and through fear of not belonging, or of others knowing the true us. And what stops us from changing the less appealing aspects of ourselves, assuming it is possible to change them, is again ourselves.

But hopefully, by the time we reach our life's end, we are most like the person we want, and ought, to be as we possibly can. For some that may mean having our own opinions rather than parroting the opinions of people with louder voices or bigger egos. We could become people who are unafraid to voice truly personal views and judgments and can justify having such views because of our own life experiences rather than taking the word of other people.

For others, it may mean making the most of our talents, however poor we believe we are in the talent department. Many famous people, including Albert Einstein, had poor school reports that suggested nothing more than a mediocre existence. A poor school performance need not label us for the rest of our lives. We change and adapt to new situations; we learn things in our own time and under differing conditions. Just because we get off to a shaky start it does not mean that our entire life is bound by the comments we get in our school reports.

For example, a single comment from a teacher may put us off that subject for life. But who is that person who labels us at a young age? Not someone who can predict our performance for the rest of our lives. He can only comment on how he perceives us at that time under those conditions. We can slough off these negative comments when we leave that environment behind if they have not been helpful ones. They do not define us for life.

At about age seven, my maths teacher wrote in my school report, 'No great mathematical brain!' I did struggle with my maths and I did remember her comment. I scraped through my O Level. But I did well at maths A Level and went on successfully to complete a degree course in physics – where I had to cope with even more maths. So, as it turned out, I probably have a more mathematical brain than my primary school teacher ever had.

Some limitations, such as a disability, cannot always be got over through effort but the way in which we deal with them can often be improved. Our attitude to a disability we may have, the way we relate to other people regarding it and by choosing our friends carefully can improve the quality of our social life. Employment is far easier for people with disabilities today than it has ever been – it is up to us to make our needs known so that employers can accommodate them. And it is up to us to remind people that we have as much a right as everyone else to a place on the planet.

Who are you?

Describing oneself requires a great deal of thought. You may need to consider the deeper aspects of your psyche in addition to superficial descriptions such as your bodily appearance or taste in clothes and music. You will need to think of the way people behave towards you (such as with respect and liking or with disdain or disapproval), things people have said about you and the ways you have behaved. Everything in your life will help to build up a picture of the current you.

Write down everything you can think of about yourself. You may need to do this over several days, or even longer as aspects of yourself will come to mind while living the life you have. Some suggestions are given below.

What are your characteristics? Perhaps you are confident and outgoing, or shy and retiring? You might enjoy picking on people or you might always be the one who likes to calm situations down and are prepared to do anything for a quiet life. You might have a good rapport with children or animals or you might be more interested in controlling other people.

Do you like company or do you prefer long periods of solitude? Are you easy-going or do you get upset if there's a slight alteration to your routine?

What do you like doing? How do you choose to spend your time? Do you like reading, walking, listening to music, watching films or football? How would you spend an ideal weekend? What would be your ideal job?

What do you dislike doing? Do you dislike your work? Do you dislike spending time with certain people? Do you dislike domestic chores?

What do you value? In other people, you might value their support and their trust. Or you might value their company. Materially you may value very little or find it important to have the latest gadgets and high tech equipment. Do you value your health? Why do you value some things and not others?

What beliefs do you have? Do you follow a religion? Are you interested in politics? Do you have firm views on how, for example, people should bring up their children? What do you believe the world should be like and how the people in it should behave?

What do you look like? It may be that you totally dismiss your appearance as having very little to do with you. You might feel that external appearance is irrelevant. But even that says something about who you are. Perhaps you are making a statement by showing other people that your appearance is of little or no importance to you. If this is so and you find acceptance by others not to be a problem then you are lucky in being satisfied with yourself.

However, if you are unkempt and this aspect of you is preventing you from getting the job you want or the partner you'd like, is this helpful to you? Do you ever look at other people with that job or partner you'd like to have and wish that could be you? Which is more important to you? Being true to your favoured form of dress or achieving what you are capable of in employment and not being lonely?

Who are your friends? The people you choose to socialise with say a great deal about you. Ed's friends smoke (and not just tobacco), enjoy drinking and spend their free time in pubs or watching DVDs and sport at a friend's house while eating a take-away. All of them work, although not all the time as they are casual labourers and pick up employment when they can. None of them has family commitments.

Other people do not judge Ed on only himself; they look at the bigger picture to form their judgment. When out with his mates, the superficial images observed of Ed drinking and smoking, sometimes in the daytime when he might have been expected to be at work, are amplified by the fact that he is mixing with others who seem to have the same lifestyle.

The messages outsiders receive could be that Ed is not ambitious and is happy to coast along in life, that he has no family or mortgage responsibilities. These are all correct. But assigning prejudicial values to Ed of being lazy or being a social parasite – assuming he is receiving a state benefit – have no grounding. When Ed has a job to do, he works extremely hard and, on the days he doesn't work, he lives off previous earnings as he generally works some time each week. Occasionally, with a big job, Ed will work several weeks at a time and then have a week or so free from work. Ed does not see himself as lazy – he chooses to live within his means and prefers the free lifestyle he has to working regular hours.

Think about your friends and what they say about you. What is it that you like about being with them or being seen with them? Are you proud of your friends? Do you think they are proud to have you as a friend? Are you a good friend?

How do you behave? You might be noisy when with friends and quiet when alone or you might go looking for trouble and try to pick arguments with your partner or friend. Are you different when at work from how you are at home? Why and in what way? Do you need to behave in a professional manner when at work? If so, how does this come across?

How do you behave with your family? When out on your own? When away from home?

How do you view your characteristics? For example, for someone who enjoys conflict, you might think it either a positive or a negative attribute. If you think it is good to be in frequent conflict with other people, it might indicate that you feel you are more important than other people.

Perhaps you lack empathy (understanding what it is like to be in the other person's situation) and sympathy (feeling you would like to help the other person in some way)?

Who should you be?

You should be someone you can be proud of and someone who enjoys being you – because no one else can be any better at it. If you are not proud of yourself, you need to do something about it.

It is your responsibility to glean exactly what it is that you want, and to work out how to get it. You owe it to yourself. And if something stands in your way, you must look until you find a way round, or adapt in some way so that you can accept the new reality. There are often several paths that lead to the same outcome: if one is blocked, the others may not be. It is up to you to try to find a way through whenever possible. This can be hard, especially if you feel you have had a shaky start in life, but you owe it to yourself to try your best.

If one of your personality traits is that you give up easily, ask yourself if that trait is getting you to where you want to be. Probably not. Are you not worth fighting for? You are responsible for the happiness of that person inside you and you must take action and try your utmost to break through things that bar your path. Life is tough enough with external hindrances without the internal hindrances of not having sticking power or of having unclear goals – or of having your past adversely influence how you are now.

Once you know what you want, the rest is a matter of time and dedication as long as what you want is not so beyond your grasp that you are hoping for a fantasy life. You need to be realistic without being pessimistic. Take a critical internal look at yourself and ask yourself why it is that you are not getting what you want out of life. Then acknowledge that if you carry on doing exactly as you have been doing, it is not likely to change what you have been getting.

Phil dutifully applied for job after job to get promotion in the company where he worked but was always turned down. Eventually he asked what it was that he was doing wrong. Reluctantly the management admitted that Phil had problems working in a team – he tended not to listen to what his colleagues said to him and would not take on board suggestions they made without enormous conflict. Phil was considered a loner in his job and loners did not make good line managers. If he had the respect of his colleagues, things would be different but the management felt he was unapproachable and would not be prepared to listen properly to colleagues' concerns.

The informed Phil now had two options. One was to ignore what he'd been told and carry on as he had been doing for the last ten years; the other was to take note and make every effort to change the way he related to other people. Which would you do?

Phil took note but knew that he'd wrecked his chances in the present company since they'd only seen his negative behaviour and he felt that his colleagues would not easily change towards him. He looked for a job at the same level where he could prove he had the skill for teamwork and then successfully sought promotion within that new company. Although it took a lot longer than Phil had hoped, he reached a managerial position in the end – and was better at the job than he would have been previously because of the changes he had made.

Divide information about who you are into two. One list is to include all things you consider positive about yourself, the other the negative things about yourself. Although none of us is perfect, to love ourselves we do need to have the greater proportion of our characteristics to be positive. If not, we are likely to have extremely low self-esteem.

Select aspects from your negative list that stop you liking and approving of yourself and ask yourself why those negative traits are present in you. For example, if you are unsympathetic, harsh in your dealings with other people or aggressive, is this how you have been treated yourself? If so, you are merely modelling behaviour seen in other people. This does not mean that this is 'you', and you don't have to be that person. You can change.

Imagine being someone whom you admire or would like to spend time with; what would that person be like? What is stopping you from being that person?

Resistance to change

Many people are resistant to change through fear – it is comforting to have routine in life. They can also be resistant to change through lack of motivation.

Any change is scary and it involves taking risk – will things improve if you seek change? If your motivation is high enough, you will overcome your fear because you will see that change is essential to your future happiness.

An example from my own life where I needed an enormous amount of motivation was the lead up to my having a hysterectomy. I have always greatly feared operations and, although I'd had several minor ones, I'd never had a major one. I was unable to live my life effectively as it was – but I was also afraid to take the step I knew I should take. So I had to find sound reasons for taking that step.

I remembered all the birthdays, parties, weddings, funerals, holidays, outings and so on that I had missed, or had found an overwhelming struggle to attend, from menstrual problems starting from around the age of fifteen. Over twenty-five years, that amounted to a great many ruined occasions. At the time I had to make the decision, every single day of my life was affected, not just a few days each month.

In my mind, an unbidden image formed that stayed with me for weeks. I pictured myself standing on a raised surface looking out into a crowd of people. They were monochrome and completely silent. They had assembled gradually, with more and more arriving daily. Each person standing before me represented a spoilt day from my past.

As the day of my operation approached, I felt like cancelling it. But when I looked out into that sea of people, their previously bowed heads, as one, were raised to meet my gaze. And I knew that the reasons for going ahead overrode all else. Every day another silent person joined the assembled group, the representatives from the past having all arrived by then, and I knew that I owed it to myself, and all those future days and important occasions, to go through with what had to be done. After the operation, the group gradually dispersed as silently as they had come and I felt a peace within me as I looked out into the finally deserted area.

I find imaging like this very powerful. Whatever works for you, you need to use it to find the motivation to improve your life. Use the rest of this book to help you make powerful changes in your life.

2

YOUR SELF-ESTEEM

He that respects himself is safe from others; He wears a
coat of mail that none can pierce.
Henry Wadsworth Longfellow (1807–82)

Your self-esteem is to do with how highly you regard yourself and how highly you think other people regard you. Low self-esteem prevents you from behaving assertively.

Aggressive people with low self-esteem may hate being made to feel small so much that, instead of trying to overcome what has happened with a reasoned spoken response, either to defend themselves or to justify their action, they hit out. Passive people with low self-esteem are less likely to stand up for themselves or fight for what is right or what they believe in. This may be because they do not consider themselves worth the effort and may well believe it probably wouldn't make any difference anyway.

Positive thoughts and behaviour can turn an ailing self-esteem into a thriving one and help you build the confidence you need to deal fairly with other people and demand that they deal fairly with you (see Chapter 4).

Where does your self-esteem message come from?
If you are lucky, over the years you will have soaked up good memories of your parents, teachers, friends, partners,

colleagues, children and grandchildren praising you. You will know you are loved by the way people seek your company, laugh with you, hug you and kiss you. You will remember the times you were told how wonderful you were.

But you might also remember bad things such as being smacked, being told to go away, being bullied or ignored, being ridiculed or scorned, or even being abused in a multitude of ways. More recently, you may have been made redundant, sacked from your job, divorced or separated, or put into a care home against your will. These things dent your self-esteem and, with each occasion that gives rise to bad feelings, the dent gets bigger. It is up to you to work at filling this dent with self-praise and well-deserved mental pats on the back (looked at in Chapter 3).

Shame
Shame is the discomfort you feel when you don't live up to what you think are other people's, and your own, expectations such as when you let someone down or fail to do something you feel you should be able to do. Some people have a hypersensitive reaction to shame, especially adults who were abused as children, making it hard to share their experiences with other people.

If you have been deeply hurt as a child and were regularly shamed by being made to feel worthless, unloved, resented, used or ignored, the effects on your self-esteem can be long lasting and devastating.

Your own expectations of yourself may be over-high if your parents alternated between being distant and very harsh in their criticism, had explosive anger without tempering it to suit the situation, or belittled you on a regular basis without explaining how you could do things the right way. This can make you adopt very harsh measures over your own behaviour and thoughts so you feel shame if you can't do something perfectly, feel responsible for others when they are not your problem and feel unable to ask others for help as you think you should be able to cope on your own.

The part of the brain that is involved in shame, the amygdala, is the same as for panic and fear, which bypasses the thinking part of your brain, making your reactions to situations that touch your shame instant and hard to control: your body is flooded with chemical secretions as you react to this powerful and destructive emotion.

As a form of self-protection you may put on a false show of who you really are, too afraid to let people get close in case they see your shame: what you are really like. However, to get over your shame, that is exactly what you need to do to a trusted few so that you realise that you are still lovable despite the knowledge of what has been done to you and who you really are. However, as you will feel very vulnerable over doing this, it should be done in tiny stages over a long period of time so that you can check that your trust has been kept and adjust to having disclosed the information.

What self-esteem depends on

Your self-esteem is not dependent on the job you have, how much money you have, how clever you are or how many exams you have passed, although you can be proud of the personal qualities that got you there. Nor is it dependent on how many children you have borne or fathered – you are not worth less because you cannot have children – although you can be proud of them and your ability to cope with the rigours of multiple parenting.

Self-esteem is about you: who *you* are and what *you* can

do. It has nothing to do with how good you are compared to some other person. It is absolute. If you can praise yourself about something, you deserve that praise. It does not follow that you no longer deserve it because you find out other people have got there before you or have done it better.

Measure your successes against yourself – that is, your personal progress – not against other people. Other people are totally different from you and what they find easy, you may find hard and what you may find easy, they may find hard.

Also, we all have different starting points. Tendayi, for example, was absolutely terrified of water and had not been near a swimming pool or a beach until adulthood. She could therefore be considered to have made the same level of progress in swimming lessons once she had built up to happily standing in the shallow end of a swimming pool as someone who had always loved water and had just learnt to swim her first width. You do not have to be perfect to award yourself self-respect and to think highly of yourself.

Significant events that lower your self-esteem include someone taking the credit for your work – the time and effort you spent doing it is devalued. Being ignored or ridiculed (for reasons such as skin colour, skin-condition, accent, lack of physical prowess, lack of intelligence, family circumstances, the clothes you wear, any obvious disability) can make you feel isolated, unwanted and foolish.

If rumours are spread about you, you might feel shamed and worthless. If no one looks pleased to see you, you might feel unloved and unvalued. If all your friends are invited to a party but you are overlooked or deliberately left out, you might feel unwanted or publicly shamed. If you have no friends, or if you lose a valued friend through an argument or bereavement, you might feel isolated and unloved.

If people forget your birthday or other important dates – such as that of your driving test or the start of a new job – or if no one asks how you are after a week off sick, you might feel you are of no consequence and may as well not be around. If you fail to get the job you desperately wanted, you might feel worthless or no good.

Under these circumstances it would be very hard to feel confident and happy and hard to push away any negative images you have of yourself: other people's behaviour constantly reminds you how little they think of you.

This may make you withdrawn and want to avoid social interactions because you are not expecting any good to come out of your relationships. So you'd be less likely to smile and show pleasure at meeting people, which would make it even less likely you'd get a smile yourself. This further reduces your self-esteem and is part of a vicious circle. The less you expect means the less you get and so the next time you expect even less still: and that's exactly what you do get.

Observe the way confident people behave in company: they are full of smiles, laugh easily and join in conversations. If you feel you could hone your social skills, learn from these people – and from watching actors on television and from characters' behaviour in books.

How you affect your self-esteem

Whether or not you feel proud of something you have done affects your self-esteem. The more often you do things you are ashamed of, the lower your self-esteem becomes, whether or not it is your fault you do them, as in the case of being sexually abused as a child.

Things you may have done that damage your self-esteem include being caught shoplifting or petty thieving, or committing any other criminal offence: you are likely to feel mortified. For some people, stealing is a manifestation of an emotional problem and they need counselling. Being publicly drunk where everyone can see the state you are in is likely to make you feel ashamed about it afterwards. Being rude or tactless to someone who didn't deserve it is likely to make you feel embarrassed about it afterwards.

Things you may have failed to do that damage your self-esteem include failing to recognise someone until after she's passed you, making it look as though you'd deliberately given her a brush off. Forgetting your or your parents' wedding anniversary or your best friend's birthday suggest you don't care about other people and will make you feel guilty, especially if friends and family always remember your important dates.

It is also embarrassing to have missed an appointment, failed to keep your temper in check or presented shoddy work and had to be asked to do it again.

Failing other people's expectations can damage your self-esteem. Very often, other people have clear expectations of how you should behave. However, these may not tally with your own personal expectations of how you should behave. If certain standards have been thrust upon you by someone else's influence, question their validity. If they are not what you personally agree with, and you cannot fulfil them, you may be unnecessarily lowering your self-esteem. Mentally check whether these expectations are reasonable. If not, don't waste time and energy trying to fulfil another person's goals.

Failing your own expectations of yourself or 'letting yourself down' damages your self-esteem. For example, if you are very religious but fail to keep to the laws of the religion or you try your utmost in exams but fail to get the grades you want or you accept a job but you find you can't cope with it. Or you might want to look different from how you actually do look, or you lie when you feel you should have been brave enough to tell the truth or you bitch about someone when you like to think of yourself as fair and non-judgmental.

You might have made a conscious decision not to have sex until you are in a very stable relationship, but you get drunk one night and have sex with a casual partner, knowing you would not have done so had you been sober. Or you might mistreat your body – by self-harming, attempting suicide, taking illegal drugs and drinking excessive amounts of alcohol – telling yourself you don't count, that you're worthless. You are not worthless but you do need help. Counselling will help you understand why you feel the need to do these things and will help you to come to terms with things that trouble you. It will help you move forward.

If you meet your expectations most of the time, you are perhaps being unreasonably harsh with yourself. If you are continually failing your expectations, partly re-write them and partly change the way you do things to make it more likely your expectations are met.

Whom you spend time with affects your self-esteem. If you spend a great deal of time, for example, in a friendship group where you are the slowest, the least witty, the least quick, the least strong, the least academically able, you will find it harder to feel good about yourself.

Similarly, if you are in a clique that has rigid rules, you might find it hard to live up to the expectations of that group. For example, in a very religious circle you may feel low if you think you don't have the same depth of faith as the others or if you find it impossible not to keep sinning in their eyes and the eyes of your God.

Self-criticism can damage your self-esteem especially if you have very high personal expectations – some of which were looked at earlier. Do not judge yourself on one incident, on one mistake alone; take yourself as a whole. You are allowed to make mistakes; you can't go through life avoiding them. No matter how hard you try there will always be a time when your guard is down. Understand that making mistakes does not mean you are worthless.

As well as criticising personal actions only known to you, you might judge yourself on other occasions through other people's knowing eyes. You are imagining what they think of you and you may, of course, be right: but you may also be very wrong. Or you may have been deliberately given the wrong message because of another factor altogether, such as jealousy.

Instead of concentrating on what other people's opinions of you are, concentrate on what you think of yourself: you know yourself far better than anyone else, so how could someone else have a truer opinion of you than you could? Yes, occasionally you need some home truths about the way you behave but this is part of your learning experience and you mustn't let yourself be crushed by it. Use the experience to grow. Real home truths – that aren't insults designed to hurt and demean you – are useful. Anything else can be discarded as not useful at all. Learn to distinguish between useful criticism and non-useful criticism.

Most of all, be kind to yourself. People with low self-esteem tend to be vastly over-critical; more so than they would be over someone else having made the same mistake. Why should you judge yourself more harshly than you would another person? Forgive yourself and try not to spend most of your life regretting the past. If you do, you may as well regret the future too. Let go of all the guilt and agonies of past mistakes and move on.

3

REPAIRING A DAMAGED
SELF-ESTEEM

To establish true self-esteem we must concentrate on our successes and forget about the failures and the negatives in our lives.
Denis Waitley (1933-)

High self-esteem is what most of us have to work at: we shouldn't regard it as a gift either bestowed or not bestowed upon us at birth or in childhood. We should see it as something that requires regular effort and attention; we need to learn skills to enhance and protect it.

However, life's challenges can make us passive and unable to motivate ourselves to seek a solution so we need to become determined to make a difference in our lives and strive each day to raise our self-esteem. As we feel better about ourselves, it will become easier to continue the work.

Reinvent yourself
Reinvent yourself in your own mind as a successful, worthwhile person with much to offer. Look at yourself from a positive perspective, instead of perhaps a negative

or warped perspective given to you by other people. This will help motivate you to become your true self, reaching your full personal potential in all aspects of your life.

To help measure your progress, write down how you regarded yourself before starting to read this book. Use descriptions you have used in your internal dialogue so that you consciously identify any damage you are causing. I have given an example below.

Gita's negative description of herself is: I am lazy because I don't go out to work, I am not a good cook, I have no special skills, I lack education, I am useless, I don't have many friends and I am not someone people warm to.

Are any of your negative descriptions owned by someone other than yourself? For example, Gita's mother-in-law told her that she was lazy and not a good cook; it was not Gita's own opinion or her husband's. Her mother-in-law also pointed out that Gita's qualifications were inferior to her husband's, despite the fact that Gita had got as far as a university education; she just did not go on to do a doctorate as her husband had done.

When you have worked out whether the negative remarks are your own or someone else's – and worked out what agenda that person might have in putting you down – write down an honest alternative description that shows you in a positive light.

Gita's positive description of herself is: I stay at home to give my children the best start in life that I can; I work very hard in the home to make it comfortable and welcoming to my family; I cook fresh, wholesome meals every day and ensure that my family has a balanced and healthy diet; I am a parent-governor at my son's school and get involved in fund-raising events; I have two very special friends with whom I am extremely close and we always support each other in times of need; it takes me a while to get to know people but I am a trustworthy and honest person.

Even if everything you write down in both your descriptions is true, you can choose the positive one to concentrate on in your internal dialogue. These are the things you need to be telling yourself about yourself to make you feel good. When things get tough, remind yourself of the positive description. Keep it in a diary or somewhere private so that you can read it whenever you feel the need.

Take every opportunity to bolster your self-esteem by soaking up all the positive things that have ever been said about you – and add these to your positive description list. Regularly remind yourself of them, especially when you feel low or doubtful of your capabilities. Mentally applaud all the good things you have done, the things you can do and the things you are good at. Use this knowledge to counterbalance the downs in life and the unkind things people say to you.

Think of self-esteem boosting as preventative – as well as curative – medicine. You are making your mind positive so that when a knock comes, you are not felled by it. Bigger knocks take bigger boosting, so you have to work harder at it for a longer period. Each time you bounce back up after a big knock, you become stronger and more resilient. And that boosts your self-esteem.

Positive things about yourself

Reminding yourself of your own special gifts also helps to boost your self-esteem. Write down all the things you can do or are good at. Below are some ideas.

I can:

- Abseil, climb, cycle, dive, horse-ride, play tennis/squash/rugby, roller-skate, skateboard, ski, swim, walk for miles.

- Appreciate all kinds of music, compose, play an instrument, sing.
- Baby-sit, bake, bring up children, cook.
- Build and repair electronic gadgets.
- Chair meetings, run my own business, handle accounts, interview people.
- Design and make clothes, draw, embroider, knit, sew.
- Do DIY, macramé, model making.
- Help others, make friends easily, make people laugh.
- Live independently, fill in forms, understand bills.
- Mend cars/bikes/motorbikes.
- Program the DVD recorder, wire plugs, understand instructions accompanying electrical goods.
- Save lives.
- Skilfully apply make-up, cut hair.
- Speak a foreign language.
- Word process, write computer programs.
- Write poems or short stories, paint.

Now write a list of all your positive characteristics. Below are some ideas.

I am:

- A good conversationalist and a good listener.
- A good friend to those in need, caring, considerate, faithful, fun to be with, loving, thoughtful.
- A hard worker, a person who never gives up, a person with stamina, a positive thinker.
- Assertive, non-critical of others, non-judgmental.
- Aware of prejudices and stereotyping, aware of the world around me, interested in all kinds of people from all races and religions and from all backgrounds.
- Clean, neat and tidy.

- Confident, intelligent.
- Not afraid of a challenge.
- Protective of myself, protective of the more vulnerable.
- Rarely bored.
- Respectful to those who deserve it (and to people I meet).
- Streetwise.
- Supportive when I see an injustice.
- Well dressed (as far as I can be with my personal circumstances).

Qualities that are to do with status, level of employment and wealth have been omitted in the above lists. If you wish to include these, think of the qualities that got you there such as perseverance and fighting for recognition as an alien in the country, rather than assuming having status speaks for itself. Having status because of the family you were born into or because your parents own the company you work for are not things you have personally achieved. If, however, you have proved to be a respected and fair employer in such an environment, it is an achievement to be proud of: you are good at managing people.

Also, just because you don't have status it doesn't mean you shouldn't have high self-esteem. If you are unemployed and you cannot find work, for example, your self-esteem would be boosted if you did something useful or interesting with your time such as voluntary work or learning a new skill. Recognising you have worth and that your time is precious makes you feel more positive about yourself, and others will consequently show you more respect.

Rewarding yourself

You need little treats to make you feel warm inside, hence boosting your self-esteem. When you don't treat yourself it is like punishing yourself for something, real or imaginary, and telling yourself you don't deserve it. The reward does not have to be anything big – just something that you like or enjoy that is solely for yourself.

Some examples are: arranging your hair differently, getting it cut and styled; buying some flowers or a plant, some new clothes or your favourite magazine; changing your bedroom around; gardening, listening to music or watching a good film; going for a walk or run, going to the pub, going to a rugby international, having a drink in a café on the way home; having a lie-in, a long soak in the bath, an early night or a take-away; phoning or visiting a friend or playing sport with a friend; reading a good book or your favourite newspaper in peace; trying out a new recipe.

You may find it difficult to treat yourself because you feel you don't deserve it or that it is selfish. If you were brought up always to think of others before yourself, thinking of yourself first can make you feel guilty. In reality, you best serve others when you are whole, happy and have high self-esteem: you can't give to others when your own needs have been ignored for so long that you feel flat and empty inside and you don't have the emotional energy to give to yourself.

It is not selfish to give yourself treats or to deny things to others when you consider the price too high. In fact, it is the opposite. It is selfish to *yourself* if you ignore your own needs. It is, however, sometimes appropriate to postpone your needs because someone else's needs at the time are greater, or more important. And then you choose, gladly, to address those needs first.

Self-praise

It is important to praise yourself mentally for any achievement, no matter how small. Think about each situation as it arises or at the end of the day. Ask yourself how you handled the situation. If you handled it well, praise yourself. If you handled it badly, ask yourself why. Then make sure that you don't make the same mistake again. If an apology is necessary, say sorry as soon as possible. Then praise the courage it took to admit to someone else that you'd made a mistake. If you had coped with something that was particularly hard, congratulate yourself on coming through; even if it was with difficulty: you still managed it.

Getting rewards from others

High self-esteem usually produces rewarding behaviour in yourself, which makes others enjoy your company more and so further boosts your self-esteem. Conversely, with low self-esteem, you get into the habit of not expecting people to enjoy your company and so have no ready smiles when someone does come up to talk to you: neither do you feel able to initiate a conversation yourself.

Try to make your behaviour more rewarding to others so that they are more likely to seek your company; and try to show others that you enjoy theirs. Concentrate on enjoying the moment, rather than worrying whether you are boring the other person – or you really will bore him. Rethink the way you see yourself and reassure yourself that you are an individual with worth and that your company is enjoyable and interesting to others.

To increase the possibility of making friends, find something that you enjoy doing and can do with others. For example, you could join a sports club or the local ramblers group, Rotary or Women's Institute. If you are politically minded you might like to join a local pressure group such as Greenpeace or Friends of the Earth. If you prefer the idea of doing something practical to help others, consider working voluntarily. The Women's Royal Voluntary Service (WRVS) helps in hospitals and volunteer hospital drivers are needed to take people to appointments. Local charity shops often need extra helpers, youth clubs may also need help, as do many church or religious-based activities. Meeting people who already have things in common with you means that you've got something to talk about, or do together, right from the start. It also gets you out of your home so that you feel less isolated.

Take responsibility for your own happiness and work at changing your life to make you feel better. Don't expect friends, for example, just to fall into your lap and stay there. All relationships have to be worked at.

Making the most of yourself

Feeling good and boosting your self-esteem are linked. When you don't feel good, you don't feel confident and your self-esteem is liable to diminish. You need to nurture yourself because you are so precious. No one can care for you quite like you.

Learn to love and like your body. Everyone has aspects of their body that displease them. Accept this and then concentrate on accentuating the good aspects of your body while playing down the less favoured ones. For example, if you have a big tummy that you feel very self-conscious about, avoid wearing tight clothes and wear shirts outside your trousers or skirts in a big enough size for them to fall over your bump rather than hug it. If you have a very wrinkled neck that you prefer people not to see, hide it with a flattering scarf or high-necked top.

Don't pressurise yourself into dieting. Sensibly reduce your intake of sugar and fatty foods if you are overweight. Make a plan of action: crash dieting leads to yo-yoing of fasting and bingeing and is not good for you – and you don't want to risk ill health or an eating disorder. Get advice from your doctor before starting any new diet regime.

Eat healthily: at least five portions of fresh fruit and vegetables each day are generally recommended. Avoid too much junk food and eat regularly: don't skip meals, particularly if you work long hours and the job requires stamina, physical effort or long-distance commuting.

Limit the damage to your body by stopping smoking – or reducing the number of cigarettes a day or drags per cigarette – by not taking non-medicinal drugs, and by not drinking excessive amounts of alcohol. Don't over-indulge in food and late night parties either. Keep yourself fit and strong.

Don't do everything in a rush. Plan your day the night before, or earlier. Organise your time effectively so that you look and feel efficient and in control. Don't rely on crisis management, performing the tasks just before they are due, reacting to things in a panic.

Pay attention to your personal grooming. When you go for an interview you usually dress very smartly, put on make-up if you are a woman, are clean and well groomed, have had a refreshing night's sleep and are well prepared. Imagine how confident this makes you feel. There is no reason why you shouldn't take extra care each day before you present yourself outside your home – get up that little bit earlier if necessary, or prepare the night before – to boost your confidence. Consult a style and colour book if you are not sure what suits you best.

Watch how other people behave. What is it that shows them to lack confidence? Remember, so that you consciously try to stop yourself from doing the same. What shows them to be confident? Remember and copy their actions, their mode of dress, what they say and how they say it and the way they do things, with modification to suit your personality and complement your personal style. Absolute copying will not necessarily show actions as genuine as they may not fit your attributes: for example, body style, way of walking, your particular voice.

Be optimistic rather than pessimistic: view a glass of water as half full rather than half empty. Don't say to yourself, 'Oh, I'd never be able to do that ...' but, 'I've never done it before but I'll give it a try.'

Taking responsibility

Learn to rely on yourself to meet your own needs: for example, if there is something lacking in your life, it's down to you to do something about it. However, don't be so self-reliant that you cannot ask others for help even when you desperately need it.

Make your own decisions – after listening to other people's advice first, if you like, to get a bigger range of choices available to you. If you don't make your own decision but do what someone tells you and things go wrong, you are likely to make the childish response of putting the blame onto someone else which will not boost your self-esteem. Weigh up what is the best option for you and then carry it out. If it happens to be the wrong choice, learn from the mistake and know that you have grown because of that experience: you'll know better next time.

Take control of your life and make things happen. Trust your own feelings and judgment: believe in yourself and know that you have the power within you to make a difference.

4

PERSONAL RIGHTS

I am the inferior of any man whose rights I trample under foot.
Robert Green Ingersoll (1833–99)

Everybody has certain rights they need to uphold to protect themselves from other people and protect their self-esteem. If you do not stand up for your personal rights, you also risk losing your identity. Your behaviour greatly defines you – who you are, what you do, what you stand for and what you believe in – and if you allow others to control this you are denying yourself the right to be you. You also need to be aware of these rights so that you don't violate other people's rights: their rights are the same as yours.

Your rights
These rights are not legal rights and so cannot be enforced by anyone but you.

I have the right for others to respect me and treat me as their equal
No one has the right to make you feel small and, if they do, they should have it pointed out to them. Do not accept

put-downs; demand to be respected and to be treated as a worthy person equal in value to anyone else, regardless of external factors such as position at work or social status.

For example, someone says to Colin, 'Not another one from that family! You're all thugs!' Colin replies, 'I think you are referring to my two older brothers. I'm the one applying for the job, not them. I have excellent references and have no criminal record.'

Imagine you have just been promoted at work. The people who are now under you had also tried for the same position and now resent your superiority over them. They keep making snide remarks about you needing to come up to scratch and wondering whether you'll cope with the job.

You could say, 'We are all dependent on each other for the success of our team. We must not let personal feelings get in the way of doing our work well. I work hard and I expect you all to as well. We all have the same aim, or should have: to excel in our field.' Here, you have ignored the comments about your possible weaknesses: it is better to concentrate on the job, not on personal attacks. And you were protecting your right not only to be treated with respect but also your right to be a success (looked at below).

I have the right to tell other people about my needs and to prioritise them
Your needs are individual to you and only you can decide how important they are to you. Therefore if something is of the utmost importance to you, you must let people know; then they can help you to fulfil those needs.

For example, two of your needs for finding a new job may be to: work close to home so that you can have a good family life and have a job where you feel valued and respected so that you can become a true part of a team making a difference to the people you work with.

If you were to prioritise these needs, you may feel that it is worth living further away from home than you'd like in order to secure the right job for you. You feel that being valued and respected in work is essential to your happiness whereas, although living close to home is preferable, you could cope with living further away if you had to.

The agency that is sending you to interviews is pressuring you to take a job that satisfies neither of your needs. You must tell your contact why you have turned down certain jobs, what it is you are looking for and on what points you are willing to compromise.

If you are well known for being helpful, reliable and dependable but feel you are now being taken advantage of, you need to let people know that you have needs of your own. Someone asks you to undertake another charity event by organising a disco. You could say, 'I would normally be happy to do it but I'm afraid that I've neglected my family the past few weeks and I've decided that I'm going to have to cut down on some of the extras quite considerably. Have you thought of asking Caspar? He's more than capable of sorting something like this out.'

I have the right to decide things for myself and am prepared to accept any consequences

You should be able to make genuine life choices: to decide what *you* want to do with your life, not what your parents, partner or anyone else want you to do with it. For example, it is up to you what career you choose, if any, and then it is up to you to deal with the consequences of your decisions and take responsibility for them. If they turn out to be the right decisions, you have boosted your self-esteem by proving to everyone you were right and that you are comfortable with what you have chosen. But if it turns out you made the wrong decision, you need to be big enough to admit it and do something about it.

All your decisions should be free of guilt and emotional blackmail. For example, if your parents never had the chance to go to university and they want you to go because they'd loved to have gone, it is wrong for them to pressurise you into going if you don't want to.

You also need to have the freedom of other life choices. For example, you should be able to choose your temporary or life partner without being criticised or others being judgmental towards you. Your own judgment should be respected. This, of course, breaks down if you are not comfortable with your own decision. For example, if you know that your partner has a history of being violent or unfaithful, it is reasonable to expect concerned parents and friends to say something. But it still remains your decision what you are to do about the situation.

Another life choice that is often interfered with by caring parents – and other people – is the way in which you bring up your own children. Your parents have had their chance of parenting and it is now your chance to do what you feel is best for your children. However, if interference is deserved – for example, if you or your partner have neglected them or abused them in some way, you will need to acknowledge this. But it remains your decision as to how you put it right, unless the children are considered 'at risk' by the authorities. Then such choices may be taken out of your hands altogether.

Try to recognise the difference between necessary intervention and unnecessary intervention on behalf of significant people in your life. For example, if you drop out of college with no goal or direction in mind you can expect people who care about you to worry and offer a multitude of advice. (Fair interference.)

But if you leave with a planned programme of, for example, apprenticeship or training and you have already ensured you have a place on a route to an alternative career, you can gain the respect and understanding of others much more easily. And you are more likely to achieve what you want. You are not just dropping out; you have made an informed decision. And you do not have to have the approval of those around you to do this. (Unfair interference.) But you do need the genuine approval of *yourself*: you must believe that it will benefit *you* and that it is the right choice for *you*.

I have the right to spend time alone and to be private

You need time to yourself to reflect on the day that's passed and to consider the day ahead. Through spending time on your own you get to know yourself better, leading to a greater understanding of your needs. People who rarely have time to themselves can lose their identity in the group structure or can become depressed because there is relentless pressure each day without relaxing breaks. You need privacy for your thoughts and some actions, and should not always be open to critical public scrutiny: this is especially difficult for those in the eye of the media.

Privacy and time alone may be possible to achieve in a busy family home – you could lock yourself in the bathroom while having a long soak or go out for a walk. But in prison, hospital or a nursing home it is impossible, unless you have a room to yourself. If you have a lack of privacy, try to concentrate on the needs you can fulfil. For example, in times of stress you might like to immerse yourself in a book of fiction – then you can be transported completely out of the world you are in and meet characters and visit places that are denied you in real life. Or you might want to start a project that you can immerse yourself in, such as making a tapestry or doing cross-stitch, model making or solving puzzles. Some people like to shut themselves off from the outside world by listening to music through headphones with their eyes closed – that gives other people a clear message to leave them alone.

I have the right to change my own mind
It is perfectly acceptable to change your mind, but it is more acceptable if it is done at an appropriate time. For example, deciding that you really don't want to marry the woman you're engaged to is quite an important thing and you must tell her you've changed your mind. But it is more appropriate to tell her one month or six months before the wedding rather than when you're at the altar or, worse still, soon after the event!

I have the right to accept or decline what others ask of me without them trying to persuade me to change my mind
Just as you have the right to make your own decisions, you also have the right to decide whether you are prepared to do something that is asked of you: it is your decision whether you say yes or no to a demand or request. Once you have made up your mind, stick to it – unless some new piece of information allows you to make a better-informed decision. People must respect your decisions, and it follows from this that they must respect *you*. Help in saying no is given in Chapter 5.

I have the right to refuse responsibility for another person's problems
You do not have to listen to everyone else's problems. You have problems of your own and sometimes those will be more than enough for you to handle. For a non-close

friend you could say, 'I'm sorry but I'm not the best person to advise you. Why don't you ask your doctor if you could be referred to a professional counsellor? They'll know about lots of similar problems. I would hate to say the wrong thing.' For a close friend you could say, 'I wish I could help. You have my full sympathy and I know that what you're going through must be awful for you. Have you thought about seeking professional help?... I *do* care about you and I'm sorry that I can't be more helpful.'

You could also be asked for practical help and here it may be simpler to refuse. For example, your friend, Ruth, has accepted a job but she has a young son who will need picking up from school and minding for a couple of hours. She asks you to do it.

Things to consider include: Ruth did not ask you before she accepted the job whether you would mind looking after her son while she works; Ruth accepted the job knowing she had a problem; Ruth cannot assume that you'll do as she asks; there is no reason why you should regularly tie yourself down to suit Ruth; this is not your problem, it is Ruth's; if Ruth has to give up the job, you should not be made to feel guilty – she should be feeling embarrassed about trying to take such a liberty with you.

Your response to her request could be: 'I understand you have a problem, Ruth, but I'm not the solution. I don't mind helping very occasionally if your son's carer is off sick but I'm not prepared to commit myself to regular minding. Why didn't you sort all this out before you accepted the job?'

Refusing responsibility for other people's problems does not mean you *always* refuse help. It just means that you choose whom you help and when. Sometimes giving help is very inconvenient but it is worthwhile for the sake of a wonderful friendship that means a great deal to you. But it does not mean that you should allow someone to take advantage of you.

I have the right to ask for something to be made clearer if I don't understand and should not be made to feel small because of it

If someone makes you feel ashamed because you don't know the meaning of a word or don't understand the question that has been asked, she is being aggressive. The person who just asked you the question you don't understand should be able to explain it to you. And if it takes more than one attempt, perhaps this person is just not good at explaining.

If you are asked a question and you don't know the answer but the questioner thinks you should, it does not mean you, as an entire person, are stupid. It probably means you didn't do your homework or you have a bad memory or you find this particular area difficult and you need more help. Don't allow one small thing to label all of you.

I have the right to ask for something I want and accept that it might be refused

If you never ask for anything, you probably won't ever get anything you want. The person who lives in hope of someone guessing his needs because he doesn't like to be 'pushy' will have a long wait. At the best of times, we are not mind readers. When we are busy and concerned with our own needs it is less likely we spend time imagining what other people's needs might be.

It might be a change in someone else's behaviour you are asking for. For example, your immediate boss at work is being unreasonable and keeps giving you deadlines to meet with insufficient notice. This means that you have to work out of office hours in order to finish in time. You could say, 'Kurt, if you gave me more notice about the deadlines I could produce better work. As it is, I'm very rushed just to finish it, let alone review it and think about it. Also, I'm getting very tired having to stay late several nights in a row because you've forgotten to tell me about the deadline until it's almost upon us. This is affecting my work the following day and my home life.'

If you want something that someone else can give you, you must let it be known – to the right person. But you also need to remember that, just because you've asked, it does not entitle you to a positive response and, when you do ask, it must be done assertively.

For example, if you think you deserve a pay rise and one is due, you have every right to ask for one. If you can tell the person why you deserve it, you might be even more likely to get it. The worst that can happen is that the person will say no. She may respect you for trying even if you are turned down. And, even if you are turned down, it does not mean you don't deserve a pay rise – the economy may be such that your employer cannot afford to give you one.

Making demands that are not deserved or sensible is aggressive and will lose you credibility so that when you do ask for something that is deserved people may dismiss your request out of hand. Asking in a passive way will be unlikely to get positive results. For example, if you make comments to your peers about it being time you had a pay rise because of all the work you've put in, you can't expect your boss to notice a rumour and act on it or respect you for it.

Don't become aggressive or become passive – such as by crying – just because someone says no. Ask for reasons for his decision but don't publicly display your disappointment in an inappropriate manner. You need to respect his right to say no.

I have the right to change any part of myself

As your knowledge of yourself and the world around you increases, you know more about the person you are and about the person you'd like to be. If these don't match up, you can decide what to do about it. You can make changes many times to the course you want your personality and behaviour to take and can make as many minor adjustments along the way as you like. However, don't have expectations that are too high, trying to reach goals that are impossible to achieve. Be kind and understanding of yourself and your limitations.

Use disappointments as good learning tools. Instead of wallowing in self-pity because you consider you failed at something, try to reverse that failure or work out ways to make yourself succeed in something.

I have the right to be myself without worrying about how other people view me

How you behave and present yourself is part of you and helps define who you are.

But if you want to deal with others without being dependent on them for approval then you have to concentrate on things that are viewed as positive in your eyes – and if you are unsure of your judgment, you could extend this to positive behaviour as viewed by the majority. This means avoiding criminal and vastly selfish behaviour. You mustn't violate other people's rights or try to harm them.

Don't mindlessly do what the rest of a group does just to feel a part of them. Do what is right for you. If you are the only one who drinks alcohol, fine. If you're the only one who doesn't drink alcohol, fine. Be the leader of your own life and get approval from yourself. Genuine self-approval is worth far more than any transitory, superficial approval someone else can give.

As well as thinking about how you behave, you need to think about the way you dress. Taking behaviour and dress to extremes, people might think (however untrue) the following:

Behaviour	*Message given*
Flirting outrageously with everyone.	You're available, unfaithful, 'easy'.
Swearing in every sentence.	Limited vocabulary, crude, best avoided.
Loud and clownish.	Can't be taken seriously, not good at keeping confidences.
Shy and retiring.	Uninteresting, boring, can't be bothered.
Screaming and shouting.	Unsympathetic, unkind, judgmental.
Condescending, superior.	Rude, believing you are better than anyone else present, egocentric.

Dress	*Message given*
Punk clothes and hair.	Non-conformist, aggressive.
Frumpy clothes.	Dull, uninteresting, boring, passive.
Displaying much expensive jewellery.	Flashy, show off, materialistic, wealthy.
Heavy make-up.	Something to hide, afraid to show her real face to the world. Dislikes her natural appearance.

However you wish to portray yourself, make sure that the image you choose is the right one for you. Unfortunately, you cannot always expect to deal with others without being dependent on them for approval. For example, when you apply for a job and are invited to interview you are very dependent on the interviewers' approval and should dress as expected. But the way you choose to dress in general should have no bearing on the way your family and friends feel about you.

I have the right to be a success
You should not feel ashamed or embarrassed at succeeding. There is no need to boast, which is an aggressive reaction to success; nor should there be a need to go to great lengths to hide success, which is a passive response to success. Share good news with the people who mean a lot to you. If others find out, so be it. Bask in any warmth you get from people congratulating you. You deserve it.

5

SAYING NO

*I don't know the key to success, but the key to failure is to
try to please everyone.*
Bill Cosby (1937-)

You need to be able to say no when the issue is important
to you. If you always capitulate and agree to things
against your personal wishes, you are pushing aside and
discounting your innermost needs, which lowers your
self-esteem.

Saying no can be extremely difficult, especially if you
want to say no to something you have always agreed to in
the past. But remember that you have a right to change
your mind.

Saying no assertively

Very often, people are forced into doing things or accepting situations because they do not like to say no or don't
say no in an assertive way. When you refuse something,
you must not leave any doubt in the other person's mind
that you do mean it.

Dawn was asked by her friend Rhys to ring up his boss
pretending to be his mother to say he was ill. She said,
'No, Rhys, it's not something I'd do and it would make me

feel bad. Besides it's risky for you – if they needed to call you about something and you weren't there, you could lose your job.'

Virginia worked in a newsagent. Her friend Diane asked her to pinch a box of chocolates for her but Virginia refused: 'No, Diane. I'd get the sack if I were caught. Maybe they'd even prosecute. I'm not prepared to take the risk.'

You do not always need to give an explanation, but it may help to clear the air and make it plain where you stand on the issue. However, if you don't want to enter into a discussion, just say no and leave it at that.

Exercise in saying no
Think of a situation where you had difficulty saying no, or a time when you didn't succeed at sticking to saying no. (Read *Example dilemma* following this to help you with this section.)

1. Write down the things that the person said to persuade *you* to change your mind.
2. For each comment, write an *assertive* reply that shows you meant what you said.
3. Were there any comments *you* said to *yourself* that helped persuade you to change your own mind?
4. How should you have mentally responded (self-talked) to these?

Example dilemma
You share a small flat with a friend called Pete and you both agreed when you took it on that neither of you would have partners to stay the night. But now Pete wants his girlfriend, Teresa, to move in with him. She's been staying over more and more which, although you turned a

blind eye to, you're not happy about.

You feel uncomfortable and unable to relax when she's around and she's spoilt your enjoyment of being with your friend. Often when she's in the flat you can hear her giggling with Pete in Pete's room. Your relationship with Pete has changed completely and now you feel an outsider in your own home.

You are also annoyed that Teresa spends ages in the bathroom and makes a mess in the kitchen, which she doesn't clear up. You cannot under any circumstances accept that living in the flat with her would improve your life.

Your friend asks: Can Teresa move in with me?
You reply: No, Pete. That's not what we agreed.

1.   Write down the things that the person said to persuade you to change your mind.
2.   For each comment, write an assertive reply that shows that you meant what you said.

Pete: I know we agreed that before but things have changed now. We love each other and want to be together whenever we can.
You: Things have only changed with you, not with me. Why don't you find a place you can both share? I'll get someone else to take over your room.

Pete: There's no reason why we can't all be friends.
You: I think that's a bit naïve. Our relationship has already changed. We don't do things together any more and you spend most of your time in your room with Teresa.

Pete: Why don't you get a girlfriend too? Then we'll both be living with someone.
You: I can't just go out and get one. Anyway, I'll choose to ask a girl out when it suits me, not you. And even if I did go out with someone, it doesn't mean I'd choose to live with her or her with me. That's not the issue here.

Pete: You're just being selfish.
You: We each agreed how this flat-share would be. It was not selfish then and it isn't now. It's how I feel. I don't like it and that was made clear at the start.

Pete: Why don't you move out then?
You: I think it's unfair to ask me to move out when it was not me who broke our agreement. I'd hoped to be treated better than that by you.

3.   Were there any comments you said to yourself that helped persuade you to change your own mind?
4.   How should you have mentally responded (self-talked) to these?

You: It's easier to agree to keep the peace.
Self-talk: I must protect my rights.
And: I must protect my self-esteem. I must not change my values because of pressure from another person or I shall lose control over my life.

You: I suppose it's not worth losing a friend over.
Self-talk: What sort of friend is he to try and push me out of my own home or go against what we'd mutually agreed? He's trying to change the rules, not me.

In this example dilemma, if Pete does not agree to move out, you have two choices. Either put up with Teresa's continual presence and renegotiate rent, etc., or find somewhere else to live.

Think what you could have said in all the situations where you felt you were persuaded to change your mind against your will or better judgment and then use the experience of these and your new responses to protect yourself better in the future.

Using saying no to regain control and respect

Sometimes it is good occasionally to say no to people for the sake of saying no. This may sound strange but many people feel they have lost control over their lives; their time is swallowed up by everyone they deal with such as partners, children, parents, in-laws, friends, employers, and any voluntary committees they may be on.

For example, if you have a friend who expects you to go out with her every time she calls, and for you to put aside whatever you are doing or had planned for the day, it would be good occasionally to remind her that you have a life of your own that is not always at her disposal. If you have established a pattern where you have always gone when she's asked, you could soften the message you give to your friend by saying, 'Actually I planned to weed the garden today as the weather's fine. How about next week?'

By explaining that you already had something planned and that it was dependent on favourable weather – which might not hold making it chancy for you to delay weeding – makes it a stronger case for your friend to accept your refusal with good grace. And by suggesting when you would be prepared to go – not the next day, but next week – you show her that you want a bigger gap between your trips out. It is also not you saying no entirely to her invitation of going out – you are just saying not now. All these things limit justification for your friend to feel offended.

I am not suggesting that you should say no to everyone every instance you are asked something. Prioritise where you would really like to claw back some time, especially time that you resent giving.

Joanne resented the number of occasions she was asked to shop for her elderly mother. Instead of thinking ahead and making a weekly or twice-weekly list, her mother would ring Joanne up most days, sometimes more than once, adding to a running list of things that she wanted Joanne to buy for her. Often she would ring to add an item just after Joanne had returned home from shopping.

Joanne sat down face-to-face with her mother and said, 'I know that you can't get out like you used to and you hate being dependent on other people for help. I don't mind giving you that help, but I do mind having to do it in dribs and drabs; it makes it harder for me to run our house and do all the things I have to do. How about if I ring you Monday and Thursday evenings to find out what you need so that I can get them to you Tuesdays and Fridays?

'If you need anything in an emergency, such as a trip to the doctor's, of course I'll take you. That's no problem. But everyday stuff can be thought about in advance. You could make a note of all the things you need as you start to run out of them and just keep adding to the list until it's one of the times to pass it on to me. If you could do this, it would be enormously helpful and will make it easier for me to plan my week.'

Joanne had kept further control of the situation by saying she would ring her mother rather than have her mother ring her. Joanne wanted to make the call when it was convenient for her so that, for example, she wouldn't have to break off while she was cooking or helping her children with their homework.

You might feel the need to say no when asked to lend money or give more money – perhaps to an unappreciative teenager. Or you may want to refuse to spend every Sunday at your in-laws', or doing repeated odd jobs for someone who can't be bothered to learn how to do it himself, or allowing a teenager to have sleepovers when she does not clear up the detritus the day after.

Saying no under these circumstances reminds people that you have needs too and that you are prepared to insist that sometimes they are addressed. If you feel this is hard for you to do, justify it in your mind before saying no, so that you are prepared to give a full explanation if asked.

You might feel the need to refuse to keep yielding to requests for working overtime. It can be good to remind people that you are in control of your time outside of work hours. Many people at work are sometimes expected to do more and more. Gone are many of the nine-to-five jobs and, the better paid you are, the more free time you are expected to yield to a company's wishes.

As Tariq got promoted in the company he worked for, his hours got longer and longer. After working there for several years, his employer expected him to become involved with giving presentations – sometimes in the evening and sometimes on the weekend. Not all were local so having to travel meant that Tariq was increasingly away from his family. Eventually he started to say no to his employer and said he must cut down. When asked why, Tariq used his wife as an excuse as he felt it was easier for a man to blame wanting to work fewer hours on his wife than suggesting the pace was too much for him. He said, 'If I am away again this month Smita's threatened to file for divorce.'

With the need to feel macho, many men are unable to decline a responsibility or an employer's expectation if it suggests they are having trouble coping or can't keep up with the pace; employers are taking advantage of the need for employees to hide vulnerability. Women employees may see their male counterparts working long hours and feel they have to compete to get the recognition they deserve, despite perhaps having more family commitments than their male colleagues. Employers will continue to expect more and more if no one makes a stand against unreasonable work hours.

Listen to your inner feelings

Your inner or gut feelings often tell you what you do not consciously know yourself. They can often give you a sense of fear or danger even though you cannot logically think of a reason for this. Your gut feelings are there to protect you and guide you. If you learn to listen to these feelings and interpret them, you often have the answer that you cannot glean through conscious consideration.

Lindsay was offered a lift home from her bus stop by a man she knew only by sight. It was raining and after dusk. Logically she thought, 'I know this person. I've seen him often enough. He works in the same building. He wouldn't risk anything where he is known.' But her gut gave a slight twist and she was aware of a warning sense of danger within her body. Did she want to be alone with him in his car? Did she want him to know where she lived? Did she want him to find out that she lived alone? Would anyone know she'd gone with him? She could either have ignored these feelings or played safe and refused the lift. Lindsay decided she'd rather catch cold than risk something nasty happening to her.

It is often a difficult dilemma whether to accept a lift

from someone. In the above case, the man was as good as a stranger so it was quite easy for Lindsay to say, 'No thanks. I prefer to wait.' When your inner feelings are screaming at you not to do something, then that decision is probably the right one. Use this inner strength to protect yourself.

Sometimes, your inner feelings are overactive, such as if you are a very nervous person or if you suffer from panic attacks. Then it is harder to make a decision. It would be unreasonable to assume that you are always in danger – such as the fear experienced in leaving the house when you have agoraphobia. It is up to you to talk to yourself and work out the logistics of your fears – and get professional help if they are interfering with your life.

Your gut feelings may also act as an inner voice to warn you not to do something you are strongly tempted to do. For example, someone else at work has told you a confidence and it would make excellent gossip. You are eager to tell your best friend, who also works in the same office, about it but your inner voice warns you not to do it because the person is bound to find out and you'd never be trusted again. Consciously say no to telling.

Saying no to sex

Some people wrongly assume that if a woman is no longer a virgin, she is up for sex with anyone she goes out with: they may even believe they have a right to it. This is false. The decision always remains the woman's no matter how many partners she has had. We are in control of our own bodies, no one else.

In some cases of sexual abuse, a person's self-esteem has been so damaged that she feels that she has lost the right to say no. She may feel that her body has been used without permission before and that she has no right to protest about its abuse in the future. This is untrue. No matter what has happened to your body in the past, you can change what happens to it in the future – although you might need the help of a counsellor to help you through this.

You should only have sex if you wholeheartedly want it, for whatever reason. As long as it is your decision alone that allows you to say yes then it is right for you. And then your self-esteem can remain intact.

Some men use the excuse that women do not always know their own mind or that they are coy and need it making up for them when it comes to the issue of having sex. This has led to some men believing that their behaviour is acceptable when to the woman it is *date rape*. If someone says no to sex, accept it at face value.

6

IDENTIFYING PROBLEMS

God grant me the serenity to accept the things I cannot change, the courage to change the things I can, and the wisdom to know the difference.
Reinhold Niebuhr (1892–1971)

Self-esteem is raised if you can reduce the number of difficulties you have. But you cannot put right what is wrong in your life if you don't know what it is that's wrong. This chapter will help you to focus on facts rather than vague feelings and half-formed thoughts.

Identifying problem areas in your life
Make a list of the things that you know are not right in your life now. A vague comment about being unhappy is not useful. Why are you unhappy? What are you most unhappy about? What aspect of something makes you unhappy? Also, identify areas in which you would like to improve and keep these to hand for when you read Chapter 7, on setting goals.

Once you have done this, you also need to think about the problems you have that you are not consciously aware of. There might be things that you feel aren't right but you can't identify what they are. To help you identify these things, start listening closely to your body and notice how it responds at different times (also see *Anchors* in Chapter 9). For example, when you sigh, tense certain muscles, start to sweat, have a headache, change your breathing, feel as though you have a stomach problem or start feeling upset, you have usually had a negative thought or image. Observe your body to recognise the changes and then ask yourself what thought or image was going through your head at the time. Once you have identified it, check whether it is realistic. If you think it is, add it to your list of problems. If it isn't, tell yourself why it isn't and stop it from bothering you by not giving time and energy in considering it.

Also be aware of what caused the thought or image: where were you at the time and what were you doing? Who were you with? What was said or done to upset you? This conscious awareness of vulnerable areas in your life can help protect you in the future. For example, if you always tend to feel bad when you're around a particular person, you can avoid that person or reduce the times you see him.

Some things may be in your power to change, others won't be. Some might, in time. Categorise your list as shown below.

Things you don't have the power to change
Think of ways in which you could adapt your thinking so that you can learn to live with permanent difficulties. One such way is by trying to find an alternative way of looking at them.

For example, people who survive cancer often say they do not regret their experience. They say it has given them an edge on life that other people don't have. They can appreciate and take enormous pleasure in very simple things. They may also decide that they don't want to be doing what they have been doing – it's time for a career change, to do something more meaningful and worthwhile. It gives them the opportunity to take stock of their life and get better value from it.

As well as changing your thinking, is there anything practical you can do to make your difficulties more bearable? Try to be imaginative by approaching this as a problem-solving exercise where you keep looking until you have found some sort of solution. However, if you find this hard to do, accept that it is your low mood that is blocking you as it depresses problem-solving skills and limits imagination. If you need to, try to find someone who could help you look for a solution. However, remember that your solution is personal to you – a solution that might suit one person may not suit another.

Common problems that can't be changed are looked at below.

You hate your home and there is nothing you can do about it as you don't have the financial resources to move. But you could make changes in your home; having a new look is very refreshing.

Go to the library and look in books about home decorating; get more ideas from home makeover programmes. Redecorate, stencil, swap curtains round, change the layout of rooms and swap rooms. Have a clear-out to make the place tidier. Put up shelves. Use a different table cover. Put up mirrors; even stencil them to give colour and brightness. If you are short of funds, you can hunt in charity shops, jumble sales, car boot sales and look for adverts for second-hand goods in local papers for different curtains, bedding and furniture.

There is also the 'freecycle' scheme that has been set up to help reduce landfills. Look on the Internet to find your local freecycle site. Once you've joined your local group you can offer and receive goods for free.

You don't like the way you look, but you are stuck with it. However, you can change your image and the way you present yourself.

Consult a style and image colour book. Ensure any new clothes you buy suit you and do you justice.

Change your hairstyle. Do this carefully and research hair magazines to help check that your new style is likely to suit the shape of your face. Have in mind what your feelings and coping strategy would be if things do not quite turn out how you'd hoped. Some risk in life is inevitable, but if you'd be completely devastated by a new hairstyle turning out badly then that would not be a 'safe' risk to take. You could minimise risk by having your changes done in stages: hair length or style changed first and then colouring, for example.

Being bereaved of a child or a partner is a terrible life event to come to terms with. Although it is very hard, and not everyone can do it, if you can adapt to the new situation and change the way you see things, it can help.

For example, some parents who have had tragic things happen to their children suddenly find they have a mission in life: to stop it happening to other children. These exceptional people were previously considered very ordinary. But very few put their experience to such positive use: this way of coping does not suit everyone. We are, after all, individuals and what might be the answer for one person won't be for another.

If you have lost your partner, you will have lost your life companion and will somehow need to change your life to cope with that. What can you do with the extra time on your hands?

You can't tell how something will affect you until it happens and people don't all cope in the same way. But what you do need to do is look for an answer that will suit you. If you have a big hole in your life, it needs to be filled. Be the author of your life and decide with what you will fill it once you are over the initial pain and shock to whatever has happened and you have started to recover. (If the hole has always been there, look at Chapters 7 and 8 on goals.)

Things you might have the power to change

If you are doubtful over whether you can make a change, perhaps the reason why you haven't already done so is that it appears to be too big a task to undertake. If so, try breaking up this main goal into mini goals.

You desperately want a partner. So why don't you have one? If it's because no one will come up to your expectations, you are being too fussy. If you are judging people on how they look and dismissing them as possible partners because of some disfigurement or disability or some other minor reason, you are limiting yourself and very likely won't find anyone. What is more important? To have a genuine loving and supportive relationship or being seen with someone whom others can admire even though on closer inspection that person might not come up to scratch?

I have sometimes had peripheral friendships that have pottered along on a casual basis, thinking that the other person is pleasant but that is all. Then by some chance either I, or he or she has had a crisis, or I have been thrown into the other person's company for a long period by chance, and I have realised how well we get on and how much we either have in common or think alike. Such things are beautiful experiences. If I had never bothered with anyone who had not instantly appealed to me, I would be missing out on some great friendships. If this sounds like you, re-think your personal rules. If you don't make use of opportunities you are given, you cannot blame anyone else. Use the resources you already have.

It is well known that many unattractive, overweight, underweight and scarred people, and people with disabilities, find partners. Personality is the main thing that counts. So, if you have dismissed relationships in any of these categories (or any other such as their job, the fact that they're divorced, have children ...) purely because of the category, think again. If you are in one of those categories, do you behave as though you value yourself and expect meaningful relationships, or does your behaviour put people off from getting to know you?

Is what you are doing any different from what you have always done? If your methods – whatever they may be – haven't worked so far, it's time to change them. And if those don't work, change them again until you get it right.

Your first goal might be to make new friends. Then you will need to make one special friend. Then you need to see what happens from there, whether that person is the right one for you and you for him or her. Even if you don't gain a partner, you could still gain a good friend.

None of these things is possible unless you put yourself in situations where you are likely to meet someone and are prepared to give the right body language to encourage the other person to strike up conversation with you, or for you to start a conversation with him or her.

You could suggest that a group of you go out for a drink together after work, you could throw a party and you could accept invitations to go out with anyone who asks you to widen your social circle.

You'd like to be happy, remembering past times when you were happy and wish you could be again. Well you can. It might be patches of happiness but that's what most people's happiness is. You can later try to join up small patches of happiness to make bigger patches and so on until you reach a comfortable stage. However, do be aware that often, when you look back to the past, things may seem rosier than they were; and you can't expect long periods of euphoria. Many people settle for contentment.

Identify the ingredients of that past happiness and try to recreate them. You can have fun again, for example, but you need to put yourself in the frame of mind of looking for fun and allowing it to happen. When you are with others, you need to lighten your mood or you will drag them down to a miserable state and they won't find your company rewarding. Try to match their mood instead. Be smiling and cheerful to get a more rewarding response. And, if you behave happy, you will probably start to feel happy.

You hate being away from home for the first time through going to university or getting a job away from home. You might be suffering from homesickness, which is basically grown-up separation anxiety (see Chapter 11). You could go back home but presumably you will eventually need to make the break so you'd only be delaying it. Although being away might be hard at first, if you stick with it you will end up being more independent and develop a maturity that is all your own. For the first time, you are developing under your own guidance without continued direction from parents or carers.

Look for five positive things every day such as: I made a new friend/spoke to someone new and we got on OK; the sun was shining; I love living by the sea/in the country/in a city; I've been invited to a party; I found my way around without getting lost; I got praised for something I did; I recognised someone I used to be at school with and it was nice saying hello; I bought myself a hot chocolate/

magazine as a treat; I saw that a film I'd like to see will be on soon; the lunch was good today; I enjoyed a television programme ...

Reason with yourself:

- 'I know it's hard now but I'll be proud of myself when I've learnt to cope with it; it will prepare me for adult life.'
- 'The friendships I make now will last because we will all rely on each other for support.'
- 'Doing this will get me the qualifications/training I need to have for the job I want. It will give me more choice.'
- 'I can make my own rules and my own mistakes and carve out my own future.'
- 'I can learn to enjoy spending time by myself.'
- 'I can do things when I want without asking permission from someone else.'
- 'I can learn to budget my own money and make my own decisions about what to spend it on.'
- 'Logically I know this is not a terrible place to be, it's just my perception of it at the moment because I feel uncomfortable about being here. Other people see it as a good place to be. I need to look for the good in being here and patiently wait for my unpleasant feelings to pass, as they eventually will.'

You are over-pressured with your job and are feeling unable to cope. If you were desperate it would be possible to change your job, but this would be difficult. It would be easier for you to try to change things from within your job.

Tell your boss that you're buckling under the load. Or, if you think she might not be sympathetic, get someone to intervene on your behalf – if this doesn't work you could go to someone else in authority. She should offer practical help such as by reorganising your deadlines, helping you to schedule your work so that it is done in stages, giving some of your workload to someone else or finding out why you're not coping with it: there may be some reason that can be put right. You need support.

Check that you are working efficiently – this is unlikely if you are depressed. Try to be very organised by writing lists of everything you need to do each day and cross off each item when you have done it to give you a sense of achievement.

Remember to schedule time for socialising each day – for example, you could sit and chat with people in the lunch hour – and for personal time alone, to be at peace and to do something you enjoy. This will help you achieve balance in your life.

When you are under pressure, you will definitely need to treat yourself each day. (See *Rewarding yourself* in Chapter 3.)

Things you have the power to change

Go ahead and change them! (Read Chapter 7 first to help you break your goals into manageable steps.) Note how good it feels to make a successful change: this will motivate you to making more changes.

7

STEERING A POSITIVE
COURSE

*There is no use whatever trying to help people who do not
help themselves. You cannot push anyone up a ladder
unless he be willing to climb himself.*
Andrew Carnegie (1835–1919)

In life, you constantly need to adapt to new surroundings,
new people, new situations and the new you. You change
throughout your life because of your deepening knowledge of yourself and the world, and because of events that
happen. You can also change by using the power within
you to effect a change in a way you choose, which is part
of your self-development.

You can develop in a positive way as long as you look
forward and try to improve your life and yourself. Some
people know where they are headed in the world from an
early age whereas many others don't have a clue until the
time to choose is upon them. Then they might panic or
make a hasty, wrong decision. You need some steering to
cope with this: you need to know where you're headed –
what your goal is – to get there.

Factors affecting goal-setting

Goals should not be the result of chance influences, nor should they be negative in nature such as deciding to avoid certain people or situations – because, for example, you might stammer or blush – as this is restrictive. Goals should move you forward so that you steadily push back the boundaries that have held you in and enhance your life in some way. However, there may be things in your life that have prevented you from achieving your goal and setting appropriate goals.

Self-knowledge

You need to know and understand yourself to have realistic expectations of where you are headed and where you'd like to be. You need to be able accurately to appraise your strengths and weaknesses without hugely over- or underestimating what you can do, so you don't set yourself unrealistic goals. In the past, setting an inappropriate goal may have been what prevented you from achieving your best.

Half-hearted goals

Although you need to be realistic when choosing a goal, it does not mean that you approach it half-heartedly as this will hold you back. Deciding you will follow a goal some time in the future, or that you'll do it when you are less tired or busy, is not positive: you could delay and make excuses for the rest of your life. You need to address your problems now. You need to be motivated to make time for something so important as your future and tell yourself that you *can* and *will* do it.

Emotional factors

If you have anxiety, depression or very low self-esteem, the way you feel about things stops you from achieving your aims, persuades you to draw back from positive active living, and encourages you to stop striving. If you are held back by deep emotional hurt or psychological distress, get professional help: that is, from an experienced, non-judgmental person who has been specially trained to help *you*.

Making false excuses allows you to blame a lack of luck, opportunity, skill and personal qualities on the fact that you have not positively progressed. You delude yourself that you couldn't have changed things even if you wanted to. Challenge the false ideas that you have and be determined to succeed – if not in one way, then in another.

Physical factors

The goals you can choose may be limited by, for example, poor health or a disability. But this should not stop you from choosing a goal of improving your lot within the circumstances you are bound.

Imagine you live at home with your partner and are fully dependent on her, for all your shopping, getting you to doctor and hospital appointments, trips to the library, etc., because you are chronically sick. She may feel resentful at having to do everything for you, particularly if she has a demanding job outside the home. Although you cannot do things for yourself, you may be able to improve the quality of your life and it may be possible to ease the burden on your partner.

Are you bored and irritable? How could you enjoy your time in the house more? What work or hobbies could you pursue from the sick bed?

Are you eligible for your GP's practice to arrange transport to hospital appointments? Are you entitled to any social security benefits? This could mean you could afford to take taxis to shops or to visit friends, relieving your partner of having to drive you there. You may also be able to pay for help in the home.

Are you too tired to read or do you have a disability that affects your ability to read? Enquire about one of the listening libraries that are run as charities such as Listening Books and Calibre and get audio books through the post (you may need a supporting letter from your doctor).

Does your partner have to buy your clothes and personal items? Could you get these from a mail order catalogue? Or the Internet? – this is an expanding market. Does your partner shop for your food? Could you get it delivered by a shop? Either from a small local shop or a big supermarket chain? You could order over the Internet.

Whatever your situation, often, if you think long and hard about a problem and discuss it with others, you will find some way to improve your lot.

Life rules

Another way of making excuses for yourself not to move on and change things is by perpetuating out-of-date rules you were given as a child. Although these rules may have had a place in your childhood – although probably not all did – look at them again and question their validity. An example might be never to travel away from home because you were told, 'You'll never cope on your own.'

By all means protect yourself from being way out of your comfort zone. But over-protection will get you nowhere. If you really want to do something, usually there is a way. Having a positive attitude helps.

Motivation

Self-motivated people do not sit at home waiting for life to come and get them but go out seeking what's needed to improve their lot, increasing their self-esteem and chances of fulfilment.

Only you can be motivated to take the positive step of changing your life. No one can do it for you. However low you feel, there is always an upward path, even if it is taken with professional help. And professional help alone is not a 'cure all'. You have to do your bit.

Do not mentally rely on some magical day in the future when, for example, all your problems will be solved by winning the lottery and having it change your life, your troubles miraculously melting away. Even if you are lucky enough to win, it is still down to you what you make of your future: and vast quantities of money do not automatically change lives for the better.

Don't waste any more of your precious life: start improving it now. Replace all your bad memories and experiences with new, positive experiences and use your potential to the full. With sufficient motivation, you can do virtually anything if well planned and set out in achievable steps. Choose goals that will tap your inner resources, things within you that perhaps only you know exist. Be bold and grab at life, as you have never done before.

Use your mind to help you achieve your goals

Don't underestimate the power of your mind. If you feel negatively about yourself and your achievements, you will have little positive power to draw upon. To change your life, you also need to change your attitude.

Positive imaging. To help you achieve your goals, regularly project an image of yourself in your mind having achieved what you want. If your goal is to be socially friendly and open to meeting new people, imagine yourself chatting to people in a relaxed and easy way in situations that are yet to come. Examples could be at the annual staff party or at a dinner party, over coffee at a friend's house, or over a drink with someone at a pub.

If your goal is to succeed at the business you are about to start up, imagine yourself being interviewed for magazines or radio shows, needing to expand your business because of success and branching out in other areas, or whatever you feel is appropriate. See yourself in a smart business suit in meetings with you looking confident and relaxed.

The more often you project positive images of yourself, the more likely it is that you will turn them into reality. You need to balance the negative images you have had of yourself for years with these new positive images that show you *can* and *will* succeed.

Overcome negative thoughts. Identify any negative thoughts you have that block you from reaching your goal. Examples might be:

1. 'I'm embarrassed at how little I've done with my life.'
2. 'If I say something, it'll come out wrong and I'll look stupid.'
3. 'I've never succeeded at anything, so I'm bound to fail.'

Working on false information like this will make your subconscious want to fail in order to prove you right: it is easier than moving forward. You must prove these thoughts wrong and replace them with positive thoughts such as:

1. 'My life's not over yet so I have time to turn it around.'
2. 'I can admit to not knowing something without it defining me as stupid. It is the stupid person who

doesn't ask for an explanation, not wanting to learn. The important thing is to be interested in what the person says. I may have a valuable contribution to make.'

3. 'I'm more aware of my capabilities and have discovered why things went wrong before. I can guard against the same things happening again.'

Ignore the negative thoughts and concentrate on the alternative, positive ones that are based on reality. They are far more useful.

Decisions and risk

You can choose paths that are very safe and secure, especially if you are a passive person; or be more adventurous, especially if you are an aggressive person: the choice is yours. If you are more adventurous, the risks increase but so do the rewards if you cope and succeed. If you take no risks at all in life, as with a very passive person, you can go nowhere very fast.

The assertive person is prepared to take some well-considered risks. She does not go full steam ahead but lessens the risks by checking there is something to fall back on if things don't go according to plan – such as aiming to be a doctor but settling for something less competitive when it is clear she cannot get the necessary top grades.

If you make no decision at all but just drift into, for example, whatever job comes along, you are being passive and making the decision of no choice, which doesn't give much opportunity to boost your self-esteem. Drifters don't succeed in what they want and may find that they get into a rut that is hard to get out of. People need a sense of purpose, something to aim for; goals give your life meaning.

Types of goal

Goals can aim for different types of things in your life such as personal or career-oriented goals and they can be of different magnitudes ranging from brief, mini goals to life-long goals. Parts or all of goals may be modified or replaced to address changing needs or circumstances.

A mini goal is a one-off, short-lived goal. Imagine you want to go to the cinema. You don't sit quietly at home hoping that someone will guess this and invite you but take the initiative and ask people to go with you.

You have a clear goal in mind (you want to go to see that film) and work at ways in which to go with someone (as that is your ideal scenario). But when no one can go with you, you modify the goal to suit the circumstance and go alone.

A short-term goal is something that will take from a few weeks to two or three years to achieve and involves repeated needs. Imagine you wish to follow a course at evening class. If you have responsibilities such as children and work, you need to make arrangements so that you'll be free to follow the course. You will need your partner to agree to taking care of the children on certain evenings and to give you time on the weekend to study. You would also have to make sure that you could leave work on time to attend the classes.

The same sort of arrangements would have to be made if you want to enrol at The Open University except the commitments would be greater.

A long-term goal could be life-long but since it is hard for anyone to predict the many things that may happen in that time-scale, a more realistic length of time would be about ten years. It involves a set of steps, starting at one point and finishing at a very different point, encompassing many short-term goals.

A simple long-term goal for a school pupil may be to aim at getting whatever grades he can, leave school and be trained for carpentry and then get married and have children.

Each step involves short-term goals, such as the step about getting married: he'll first have to date girls to find the one he wants to share his life with and then persuade her to marry him. Then there are more hurdles to get through, leading up to the wedding, involving both sets of families and the practicalities of where and how they are going to live.

Making a plan of action

When you make a plan of action, you have to make decisions that will move you forward in some way, such as: making you more secure in your present position; making your personal life more fulfilling; seeking a promotion at work; improving the relationships with your friends or family, or battling against poor mental health such as being treated for obsessive compulsive disorder.

Whatever you choose to do, or wherever you want to be, it must be something positive and something different from what is happening now. It must not be something that is perceived as a step back or staying in a safe rut. For example, *choosing* to be on the dole all your life is not a positive plan of action. *Choosing* to live at home with your parents all your life again does not move you forward.

Making a (long-term) career plan

This is to do with exams and qualifications leading to jobs and careers. Make your plan of action realistic. You can't expect to be a top singer if your singing is dreadful, or to be a concert pianist if you can't play the piano, or to be a policeman if you're too unfit . . . Think of where you are now and where you want to get. Then divide this into *mini steps*, breaking up all the things you have to do, in small parts, in order to reach your goal.

To jump from studying GCSE Biology to being a vet with your own practice is too big a leap. Someone with a faint heart would give up before he'd started – or have it as a distant goal that never materialises simply because he hasn't addressed the facts of what he needs to do to be a vet with his own practice.

An example action plan for the above goal is:

1. Find out which GCSEs with what grades I need.
2. Get the required number of GCSEs in the right subjects with the right grades.
3. Find out for which exams at 16+ I need to study.
4. Get a place at school or college and start studying these subjects.
5. Find out about universities. Which offer a suitable course? Which require the highest and lowest grades?
6. Apply to universities with a range of entry requirement grades so I have a safety net if I don't get the grades I hope for.
7. Get the required number of sixth form level examinations in the right subjects with the right grades.
8. Get work experience in a vet's practice.
9. Get funding to support myself while studying.
10. Follow my university course.
11. Get my degree.
12. Find my first relevant job.
13. Get experience.
14. Save money.

Breaking your main goal into many little ones helps you to understand what you need to do to reach your goal – and to recognise whether it is achievable for you. You get a sense of achievement each time you succeed at a short-term goal and this provides the motivation for you to strive for other successes, knowing that you're still on track for your main goal.

Changing direction. If you fail a much-needed exam, or something else doesn't work out, you can either try again, or if this doesn't seem likely to work, rewrite or replace your main goal: change direction. As long as you have a direction, you can repair little hiccups and recover any lost self-esteem. Just don't let the situation beat you. Get up and start over again.

Often, because of cutbacks and redundancies, you cannot stay in the career for which you were originally trained and have to change direction mid-life. Or it may be something altogether different that makes you need to change career such as a sudden disability or illness.

8

PERSONAL GOALS

Make the most of yourself, for that is all there is of you.
Ralph Waldo Emerson (1803–82)

This chapter is to do with the sort of person you'd like to be. Personal changes that are made gradually are more likely to stay with you because doing things in small stages makes it easier for the change to become permanent. Allow yourself time to change so that you get to know yourself and become comfortable with yourself at each stage.

Personal quality goals

What personal qualities are important to you? Choose positive qualities: *wanting* to be shy or aggressive or mean is not allowed. Rank your preferred personal qualities in order, then work out ways to tackle the problems of achieving them, but be realistic. Don't expect to behave like a saint. If you set goals that are too high, you'll never achieve them and then you'll damage your self-esteem. Choosing goals that are too low also damages your self-esteem because you haven't really worked at anything so cannot be proud of your achievement.

Wanting to be more sympathetic

If you brush off other people's problems too easily, can't be bothered to take the time to listen and are very impatient with people, you may find this loses you friends and creates problems between you and your partner, if you have one. You could decide to try the following as your action plan:

- Give time to anyone who looks distressed.
- Accept that if the person perceives she has a problem, it's a problem whether or not I see it as one.
- Listen to what she has to say.
- Try to think of one or two things to help.
- Show that even if I can't help, I am sympathetic.

Wanting to gain respect generally

If you feel you are not getting the respect you deserve, you might not be given credit for the personal qualities you do have. One reason for this is that people may not know what you do. If, for example, you don't share your experiences with others, they will not be aware of your strengths – such as being able to follow complicated knitting patterns or fund-raising for charities – and so you will lose out on gaining increased respect.

Another reason for lack of respect is that you need to understand that it is not freely given since most people feel respect has to be earned. Respect may be lost if you do not treat others well, or if you frequently make silly inane comments or, for example, you behave like a giggly schoolgirl, or a teenage hooligan, in your forties. If you feel that you do not get the respect you deserve from the people around you:

1. Write down why this might be – and be honest.

2.   Consider what you have done to lose people's respect.
3.   Consider what you have failed to do to win respect.
4.   Think of people who *are* respected and write down examples of their behaviour that earn respect. Can you do similar things?
5.   Consider whether you have fallen short of your own, and other people's, expectations. If so, in what way?
6.   Write an action plan, remembering the points you'd written down, of how to win respect. (This does not mean becoming a 'yes' person.)

Suggested action plan

- Take any complaint about me, or brought to me to sort out, seriously, and get details and discuss with the person what might be done, if appropriate.
- Listen carefully to anything that is said to me and respond to what the person says, not to what I think he says.
- Volunteer to do extra work such as offering to take the minutes of a meeting – either in paid or community work.
- Do a task no one else wants to do – it would get me noticed as being willing; no boss likes to see people doing only the bare minimum.
- Take extra care over the presentation of my work. Ensure, for example, there are no spelling mistakes or rough edges that need to be filed down; I should take pride in my work.
- Take the initiative. I shouldn't always wait to be asked; I should anticipate needs.
- Be noticed as an efficient, responsible and hardworking person.

- Try to be well organised and not rush to do things at the last minute. I should be in control.
- Be aware of others around me. Do they need to be reminded of an important impending meeting? Do I ever praise them? Do I ever offer help when I know they are in trouble?
- Be prepared to spend time explaining things to others. Then they will come back to me for help and others will see that I'm approachable and will respect my knowledge and experience. I should show I know what to do and how to solve problems.
- Be understanding of other people's mistakes. They will then look upon me more sympathetically should I make an error.
- Criticise someone privately if I have to, so that he does not lose face.

Always keep your personal quality goals at the back of your mind so that you use every opportunity to achieve them. But don't go all out to improve one quality at the expense of another. For example, if you want to be kind, don't do everything someone asks of you just because you want to be seen by everyone as kind: then you'd be seen as a doormat and lose people's respect.

Self-improvement goals
It is rare that someone is completely satisfied with himself: there is always some niggling part that doesn't quite come up to scratch.

Although most of this may be out of your control – for example, you can't have children because you are biologically incapable of it or you want to be a builder but have a bad back – there are things you can do. However, you cannot change overnight in twenty different ways. Work at one thing at a time and aim for steady, permanent improvement. Trying to tackle too many things at once will make you feel overwhelmed by the tasks and will lower, rather than raise, your self-esteem.

Tailor any goal plan or action plan to suit your own needs. Make it as personal as possible, so that it is very relevant to you. Update it whenever necessary. It may help to decide beforehand what rewards you will give yourself for each achievement. This helps to increase your self-esteem and motivates you to carry on.

Coming to terms with your shortcomings
It is always hard to admit there are things about yourself that you do not like. Some things you are unable to change and must learn to accept. Other things you can do something about, or at least try to improve even if you cannot do away with them altogether.

For example, if you have a rotten temper, it might be unrealistic to aim for getting rid of it completely. But you could try to limit its use to the worthiest of occasions. You could draw up a list of situations where you would try not to lose your cool. Alternatively, you could aim generally to tone down your anger (also see Chapter 10).

Other behaviour that may need addressing might include anxiety disorders mentioned in Chapter 11. If something is affecting your everyday life, you will need to seek professional help. The start of the goal to changing this side of you is to admit you need that help. The next step is to make and keep an appointment with your doctor who can refer you for appropriate help. However, if you feel that your problem doesn't play such a big part as all that but you still want to do something about it, try writing a plan of action for yourself.

If you have agoraphobia (also see Chapter 11), you might

make an action plan such as this:

1. Enlist the help of a friend to come out with me, staying out longer each time and going further each time.
2. Start doing some of these things by myself.
3. Plan to go places with a friend that require me to stay a set length of time such as shopping, going to the cinema, having a meal out, taking a journey on public transport.
4. Try to go shopping on my own – buying only one item each trip and increasing from there until I can do a full family shop. My friend could initially wait outside the shop for me until I am able to do it completely by myself.
5. Try taking short journeys on public transport and gradually increasing the length of time I travel.

Following this kind of plan is using desensitisation as a way of improving your difficulties and is a behavioural technique used in cognitive behavioural therapy (see Chapter 14).

If you know that you are ignorant about world affairs and feel ashamed that you can't join in with conversations the people around you have, make an action plan to develop your mind. If you really want to be more conversant with politics and current issues, your action plan could consist of the following steps:

1. Listen to the news every morning before college/work/housework.
2. Read a daily newspaper.
3. Put a world map on my wall and find all the places mentioned in the news.

4. Make a note of all the places people talk about that I
    know nothing of. Then locate them on my map and
    try to find out about them.

5. Go to the library and find a book on current affairs
    or a simplified explanation of how troubles have
    come about in certain areas: for example, Northern
    Ireland, the Middle East and the Balkans. Or look
    them up on the Internet at home, at work, at a net
    café or the library.

6. Look in the television pages for classes, such as The
    Learning Zone, BBC2, on certain subjects I feel I
    should know something about. Record them and
    watch them at a more convenient time.

7. Try to have some ideas of my own on how something
    could be resolved or on what comments to make
    about the war atrocities that have been happening.
    Then try them out on other people by joining in with
    their conversations.

By this time, you should be rewarded by the respect people
show when they can talk to you as an equal, no longer
having to explain everything to you. You may have even
surpassed their knowledge and understanding.

9

HELPING YOURSELF TO HEAL

When we are flat on our backs there is no way to look but
up.
Roger Babson (1875–1967)

When having to deal with past and present unpleasant
experiences, it is helpful to have some strategies to protect
you from further hurt to prevent current emotional pain
becoming deeper and to allow past emotional pain to heal.

Creating social security
Sixteenth-century-born English poet and clergyman, John
Donne, wrote (Meditation 17):

No man is an island, entire of itself; every man is a piece
of the continent, a part of the main. If a clod be washed
away by the sea, Europe is the less, as well as if a
promontory were, as well as if a manor of thy friend's or of
thine own were ...

Since his death, Donne's words have been widely published
and quoted. It is clear what he meant: we do not live in
isolation, cut off from the rest of the human race; we are

all interconnected; we all need each other. We are weaker if less connected but stronger if we are more connected. It is through developing connections we become sturdy and solid individuals able to weather storms and not get washed away by a fearsome tide.

The hot air balloon

Imagine you are a hot air balloon whose basket is anchored to the ground by ropes of varying lengths and thickness, which represent your relationships. There is one very thick rope that anchors the middle of the under surface of your basket directly to the ground. It is shorter than all the others but is the thickest and represents your strongest relationship tie that might be a parent, child or partner.

For some of you, it might represent the strength of your faith: you may gain emotional support from the many you meet through religious gatherings. However, having a strong faith that you rely on entirely where you do not have social contact with others in the faith is risky because, for example, if no one misses you when you don't turn up, no one will know when you feel down or when something happens to you; or you might have a crisis of faith without any social support to counteract the empty feelings this can promote.

Other thick ropes that connect the underside of your basket to the ground represent your most intimate relationships with others. If your strongest tie that connects you to the ground is for that of a child – or you may have several such equally strong ropes because of having several children – then your next strongest can be for your partner and parents. Very close friends can also give you fairly thick strong ropes with which to anchor your balloon.

There are also thin ropes attached to the sides of your

balloon's basket, representing less close friends and perhaps people you know well from work and with whom you have regular contact.

Transparent fibres also connect your basket to the ground and represent casual contacts you have, such as seeing a neighbour to say hello to or people at work to whom you make passing comments. The more you have to do with these people, the less transparent the fibres become. If your relationship with someone flourishes, the transparent fibre can become a rope. If there is a gap between your social contact with any one person, the transparent fibre breaks but can be reformed when the acquaintanceship is renewed. The transparent fibres are so fragile they do not offer stability to your balloon but have the possibility of becoming stronger if you allow them to.

If someone dies, the particular rope representing his friendship with you breaks and can never reform. You will have lost his support and the rope is no longer there to help anchor you to the ground. How you deal with this loss may depend on the strength of the other ropes. One rope in particular might thicken as a friend spends more time with you than usual but it could return to its former size after the crisis; or it may remain at the new thickness, the experience of greater intimacy making you both realise that you gained from increased contact. In time you can also form another new rope to fill the gap in your life left by the person who died.

If your relationship with someone becomes damaged, the rope that represents that friendship frays and becomes thinner. It may be very vulnerable at a particular point and if you don't take steps to repair it by making amends, the rope may break. You need constantly to check the status of your ropes and fibres. If a rope is frayed, repair it; if a fibre is one which you'd like to make into a rope, do it.

If you can predict the strong wind of a crisis looming – and this may not be often as most are unforeseen – you know that you will need to make your bonds stronger and have more of them. If you know, for example, that your best friend whom you rely on a great deal is moving away, you know that that rope will become much thinner. To keep your balloon stable, you will need to compensate by making one or more thin ropes thicker or by changing a fibre into a rope or by making new fibres with a view to changing them to ropes. This is all best started before the thick rope of your best friend thins. To keep your balloon very stable, you will need many ropes of varying widths.

It is the ropes that keep your balloon steady and secured to the ground. Without strong enduring relationships, you can weaken your anchor to the ground, making you in danger of losing touch with, and becoming detached from, all those around you. This makes you vulnerable to depression and presents a risk of suicide should your hot air balloon lose its anchorage completely.

Make a list of all the people involved in anchoring your hot air balloon. Then rate them out of three, where three is the most and one is the least, in terms of how supportive they are to you. This will indicate who you can rely on when the going gets tough.

Now rate how supportive a friend you think you are to these people. If your rating is lower than theirs, you risk losing their friendship or risk reducing their willingness to support you. If your rating is higher than theirs, perhaps you are doing too much for other people while neglecting your own needs. If your ratings are equal, then you have well-balanced relationships.

If you regularly need far more support from other people than you can give in return, you are overburdening your friends with your troubles. If you need major emotional support on a continuing basis, you should ask for a referral from your doctor for professional help. You might also benefit from medication while you are waiting for that additional help.

Rope challenge: the next time you go out, collect as many transparent fibres as you can by interacting with the person who sells you the train ticket or the newspaper or your daily/weekly shopping. You can do this by confidently walking up to the person, making eye contact and smiling before you get there, looking pleased to see her and saying hello. When you are given your ticket/receipt/change make eye contact again and say thanks and goodbye.

These are the easiest things to do. When you feel confident about doing that, talk to someone in a shop – you could ask someone if she's tried that particular type of orange, as you don't want to buy sour ones, when you see her pick one up. If someone talks to you, answer in a friendly way.

No matter how we currently feel, life is more manageable and more rewarding if there are other people to share it. When things go wrong, friends are our safety net – and our anchor. The safety net saves us from a rocky fall and the anchor prevents us from going adrift, from losing touch with humanity altogether, from being in a state of depression or even by committing suicide.

Creating a haven of safety

When something bad has happened to you, it is natural to want to find a safe place to stay while you recover or consider your next move or adapt to the new situation.

Neelam, for example, witnessed a horrific accident where a speeding car mounted the pavement and killed a child. The driver was badly injured. It was up to Neelam to get help and return to the scene to do what she could for the driver until the ambulance arrived.

Seeing the child's distraught mother was so disturbing that Neelam, once home, took the next two days off work and kept her toddler home from nursery: she felt the need to keep him close and out of possible harm. Although Neelam didn't realise it at the time, it also served as a protective mechanism. Subconsciously, Neelam realised that she could not cope with further trauma, no matter how slight. So while she felt at her most vulnerable she ensured that, while she recovered her equanimity, nothing else bad could happen.

When you want to find a safe place to stay, it might not be somewhere that you can easily get to. You might not, for example, favour the place where you currently live as the place you have felt most safe and calm in your life. The most restful and comforting place could be a place from childhood that no longer exists because someone else lives there now and the people you were with are dead or have moved away. However, you can reach it again through your imagination and this then has the benefit of always being available to you in times of need.

Close your eyes and imagine you are in your favoured safe place. Remember how it looked. If it's a room, look around with your mind's eye at all the things that are there. If it's a place, look around to see the buildings, plants and trees.

Perhaps you cannot think of a safe place based on reality. That doesn't matter. Imagine how your ideal safe haven would look. It could be, for example, a sunny cove in a lonely spot with a small sandy beach that is lapped at by gentle waves from a shimmering blue sea.

Wherever it is, real or imaginary, past or present, savour the smell of the place, the atmosphere, the silence and peace or the familiar noises. Note the textures of the objects around you. Are they rough or smooth, cold or warm to the touch? Are the edges sharp or rounded? Are the objects small and light enough to lift or are they too heavy to do more than run your fingers over the surfaces?

What are you doing in this special place? Lying cosily in bed? Propped up on cushions on the beach? Reading a book? Is there anything that you can add to enhance your feelings of tranquillity in the place? Soothing music? Some scented candles or incense sticks? A wind-chime that plays softly in the breeze of an open window or from a branch of a nearby tree? Are there any objects you'd like to add to this special place? Photographs? A cuddly toy? A box of chocolates? A gift that has a particular meaning for you? Your pet – past or present?

Now that you have made your safe place into the most desired place for you to be when you are in need, imagine it in its entirety. With this picture in your mind, think about how you feel in this place and what you think about it. Some suggestions are: I feel protected; I feel calm; I feel at peace; I am secure; I am safe and sound; I am free of threat; I am out of harm's way; I am in a safe harbour; I am sheltered; I have a refuge; I am shielded from harm.

Using these ideas, sum up in one sentence or phrase what your safe place means to you. Suggestions are: I am ensconced in a haven of peace and serenity; I have a sanctuary that is free from threat and shields me from harm; I feel serene and at peace in my secure and quiet refuge.

Practise creating a strong image of your safe place in your mind and say your chosen sentence in your head so that, whenever you feel the need for succour, you can quickly bring the place and your feelings of peace and security to mind. Immersing yourself in this special place and strongly associating words and feelings of safety and peace will help you heal in times of trouble and difficulty so that, even when you are physically unable to reach your safe place, you can be there in fantasy, having the image assist you through a challenging life. You may also find that spending time in this place at bedtime will help you fall asleep more quickly and more restfully.

Weeding your garden

You can regard the people you know, and the things they do or say, as your garden of experiences. Some of these people are helpful in how they behave towards you and the things they say. Consider them as beautiful flowering plants. Other people hurt you by what they say and do. Regard these influences as weeds that stifle the beauty of your garden and whose thorns hinder your progress through your garden – and your life.

To identify the weeds, divide your experiences into two columns: those that help and those that don't. Some suggestions are given below.

Helpful	Unhelpful
My partner's support.	Being misunderstood by my parents.
Being with my best friend.	The lack of acceptance in other people.
The kind words Rachel said to me.	The unkind gossip someone spread about me.
The love of my children.	My brother's jealousy of me.

Helpful	Unhelpful
The smile Adam gives me.	Lisa breaking my confidence and destroying my trust in her.
My dog's company.	Having impatient in-laws who are not willing to give me time to do things my way.
The joke Morris and I shared.	Being ridiculed for saying something stupid.
My time in prayer.	Not being missed when I was off work ill.

Now weed your garden by either ending relationships that damage your self-esteem and make your life harder to bear, or by reducing the amount of time you spend with people who make you feel bad. This may be hard to do if, for example, they are relatives. If you don't want to cut them out of your life completely, don't spend so much time with them and don't give them insight into your vulnerabilities. This can involve being scant with the truth and by omitting things: this is not lying as it is withholding information others have no right to know. You have every right to do this to protect yourself (also see *Letting go* in Chapter 19).

If you don't fill in the gaps weeding your garden has created, the weeds can quickly return and flourish. So, where the gaps are, do more of the helpful things – either by spending time with people who make you feel good or by doing more of the things that are helpful to you.

Strengthen your belief in yourself by creating a sentence that sums you up. Some suggestions are: Against all the odds, I have won through and am still here and deserve to be here; I am a fighter and a winner in my own life; I am a person worthy of my, and other people's, respect; I am a kind, considerate and caring individual who deserves to be loved.

Re-filing your memories

Once something has happened it can never be changed. But the way you feel about it can be changed by manipulating your memories.

First, work out how you store your memories. Do you see a film clip or a photograph in your mind's eye? Or hear the words or sounds? Or do you remember how hot it was and how still the air was? Perhaps it is a mix of all of these?

You might visualise the scene with you in it while observing from outside your body. In this memory, you are said to have dissociated from yourself. In a memory where you are associated with it, you only see what you could have seen at the time rather than from an observer's see-all position – and so you don't see yourself in the scene as a separate person.

A technique used in neuro-linguistic programming (NLP) for dealing with painful memories is to file them differently in your mind to make them less powerful images. For example, replace the colour with black and white: it is then less vivid in your mind. Now make the image smaller, as though you are looking at it from afar. Very often, when we remember something terrible, we picture the scene as though we are still a part of that scene. Try looking at the scene from the side or above. Choose whichever angle gives the less impact.

Re-file your small black and white image so that whenever you recall that incident, you recall this new image and not the previous one. It may take a while to get used to this new picture but if you frequently recall this one rather than the old one, you will eradicate some of the power the old one had over you. Besides, it was not true power that the image had. The emotions that it evoked in you were the problem: the image itself is nothing more than an empty picture. The people in it no longer exist: even if they are still alive, they are not the same people today as they were then.

Voice memories can also be edited NLP style. If you recall scenes more as sounds than images (or perhaps you use both), you can change the sound of the voice to remove the power it has over you. You can make it louder or softer – try both ways and pick which one has the least impact; you can distort the sound as though listening to it under water or give it a ridiculous make-over by making it sound like a cartoon character.

Going through your most painful memories and re-filing them after appropriate editing will help you when you next recall the incidents: they should have much less effect on you than previously, allowing you to get on with your life.

Now that you have dealt with unpleasant memories, spare some thought for your positive memories. You can experience a memory more intensely if you are strongly associated with it – imagine yourself in your body seeing what you saw then and hearing, seeing and feeling what you did then but also exaggerate the experience further by turning up the volume, the light, the brightness of the colours and having the images in close-up. It is best to manipulate good memories in this way to use as a resource for 'anchors'.

Anchors

An anchor (so named in NLP literature) is an automatic trigger that affects your mood in a positive or negative way. It is a learned, often subconscious, programme to which your mind and body instantly respond, and can have powerful consequences because it operates subconsciously and is not based on rational thought.

Identify your negative anchors by deliberately seeking the cause of sudden downward mood changes to help you understand why your mood changes for the worst at certain times and to reduce their effect – by changing the way you view the memory.

The triggers can be: physical – perhaps due to low blood sugar; a change in the acidity of your blood from hyperventilation; fatigue, opening the doors to a massive lack of confidence and panic while you remember previous times you felt out of control and unable to cope; visual – seeing a dog of the same breed yours was before he died, or the derisive expression on someone's face reminding you of when it happened with someone you loved; auditory – a song you were listening to when a friend got run over, or an accent someone has reminding you of your partner who has died; touch – someone touching a certain part of your body reminding you of the person who sexually abused you as a child, or the touch of velvet reminding you of your late grandmother's ball gown.

For many of the negative triggers you will be able to remove their power just by refusing to respond to them – it is easier now you understand how anchors work. But some are stronger and need more to diminish them – see *Re-filing your memories* above.

Identify your positive anchors by noting memories that make you feel good. By organising their use, and making the anchors very deliberate, you can make them work for you in a very positive way.

Find the best memory in each category – such as the memory where you were the most confident, felt the most loved, were the most successful, the strongest, the most powerful, and the most in control. Now you need to enhance them to make them powerful tools in times of need.

To create a very positive anchor to, for example, increase your confidence, remember a time when you felt extremely confident. Associate strongly with yourself – see the scene from your own eyes, not as an impartial observer, and see what you saw then, hear what you heard then and feel what you felt – and make it a bright, colourful close-up as described above in *Re-filing your memories*.

When the intensity of the memory reaches its peak, have a phrase that you associate with it such as, 'I am very confident.' Choose a discreet physical gesture, to use at the same time, that is unique to your everyday gestures such as touching your hand to your thigh, closing forefinger and thumb to form an 'O' or squeezing your fingers together. You have now created a very positive and deliberate anchor. Before it can be used to help you, it needs to be well established by practising firing it: recall the memory in full, make your unique gesture and say the phrase you chose. When you use a well-established anchor, you should be able quickly to change how your body feels for the better.

You can store many positive anchors for many different positive feelings as protection for when you feel vulnerable. Then you can call them up to help you overcome doubts or fears to give you the knowledge that you are a capable person and that you can do it.

Part Two

The Distressed Self

A will finds a way.
Orison Swett Marden 1850–1924

The amount and type of stress each of us can cope with varies from individual to individual (depending on personality, heredity, upbringing, life events ...), but we all have a threshold beyond which we can become emotionally distressed. The distress may be so great that we cannot continue at all with our everyday lives – we call this a breakdown – or we cannot continue effectively, having, for example: unrestrained anger, increased anxiety, panic attacks, and depression. We may try to struggle on, relying on medication and/or alcohol to see us through but these can lead to further problems without the underlying problems being helped in the long term.

Part Two looks at the forms emotional distress can take and gives suggestions about what can be done to help, including therapy with professionals.

10

ANGER

The man who gets angry at the right things, and with the right people and in the right way and at the right time and for the right length of time, is commended.
Aristotle (384–322 BC)

Anger can be expressed in a number of ways. Verbal abuse involves swearing, name-calling, putting-down, and verbal bullying. Physical abuse includes hitting and punching, physical bullying or intimidation, and rape. Vandalism involves destroying items. Self-harm includes cutting yourself, starving or bingeing, over-eating, over-drinking, taking illegal substances, solvent sniffing, and deliberately isolating yourself from others. Stealing from shops or other people can also be a sign of anger, wanting to hurt other people whether or not personally known to you.

Although these things may give temporary relief from frustration and excess energy and show others that you are hurting, they are not positive ways of handling anger. Angry people are more likely to have low self-esteem and less intimate relationships than non-angry people; being frequently angry is also bad for the heart.

Why are you angry?

There may be many contributing factors as to why you are angrier than most people. Some suggestions are given below.

You may have an angry personality or one that is intolerant of things going wrong, believing that you have a right to have things go your way more than other people, reacting with criticism, a need to control other people, cynicism, aggression, hostility, etc. When things don't go your way, try to see that this is not because you are unworthy of having things go right, but that things going wrong are only that – they have no special significance in relation to your worthiness.

You may have learnt to be angry from your upbringing. Did your parents punish you for being angry? Did they shame or blame you for your anger? Were you expected to obey demands without question? Were you punished without being allowed to explain your side? Were you treated violently? If you come from a family that finds it hard to express feelings verbally, you are not likely to know how to handle your feelings; not talking about them makes you frustrated without any let-up of pressure.

Society tells you that anger is a negative thing and that you should hide it. This can make you feel guilty about expressing it even when it is justified to have angry feelings. Not seeing other people handle their anger because they hide it can compound your inability to handle anger constructively.

Your life may have been tough and you may have had much go wrong. You may have often been hurt or betrayed and this can make you feel like lashing out at others to hurt them too. You may have lived with angry people and so have learnt to act in an aggressive way, or you may have seen someone react violently to a situation and so react in the same way when something similar happens to you.

Low self-esteem makes you more likely to react to situations that upset you in a very negative way. Think how differently you behave when you are feeling good about yourself and how you behave when things have gone wrong: you can handle things better when you are feeling emotionally strong.

Feeling out of control when too many things happen together, or there is a situation you feel unable to handle, can make you feel vulnerable and frightened and you might take out your frustration and anger on other people, or even yourself. It is well known that pressurised people, especially girls and women, can develop eating disorders (see Chapter 11) as a way of controlling one part of their lives because they feel out of control with all other aspects of their lives.

Bottling up feelings is not possible in the long term: they all need to be expressed at some stage. Even someone who is normally very passive but has been taken advantage of repeatedly – or has been abused, bullied or intimidated – can eventually snap. A tiny event may trigger a huge response from you as 'the last straw' because you cannot handle anything else going wrong. It is better to divulge angry feelings early in a controlled way rather than letting them explode out of you in a very destructive manner.

Living in emotional isolation denies you an outlet for your feelings: you won't be able to discuss events that have happened with another person to see alternative viewpoints or solutions or to discuss ways of handling the situation. This makes you more likely to have difficulties in dealing with your feelings.

Dealing with your own anger

If you know that you have a low tolerance to anger – whether showing it outwardly or letting it boil within you so that you are constantly grumpy and irritable – you need to address the problem as it will interfere with your relationships, giving you more cause for frustration and irritation and making you more prone to depression or becoming physically ill.

Note which buttons other people press. Work out what causes your anger so you can take steps to manage it. If you have vulnerable areas that people regularly touch on, consciously work at finding a way to protect them (see Chapter 4 on personal rights).

Note the times you're vulnerable to anger. Are you angrier when you feel unwell? When things have gone badly for you at work? If so, let people know that you feel vulnerable at these times so that they help you by being more careful in what they say and do. However, you cannot plead having a bad day every day and expect people permanently to bow to your caprices – but if you genuinely do have a bad day every day, address the things that are causing it.

If you are always tired at night and that's when the arguments start, arrange to talk about things that are important to you when you and your partner are feeling good. If certain routes make you angry because of other drivers, change routes or change the time of day at which you travel, or change your method of transport.

Change the way you think. Note the things you say either aloud or to yourself when you are angry. These may include swearing, highly emotive language such as, 'I'll never forgive you for this' and, 'That's the last time I'll do anything for you', and mentally exaggerating the event out of proportion.

Using words like 'never' or phrases like, 'You always ...' are negative and accusing. It makes the situation worse, fanning the flames of your anger and igniting the other person's anger. Talk about what's happened; discuss why things went wrong and what can be done to try to ensure it doesn't happen again otherwise you risk alienating the other person, creating hostility instead of fostering co-operation.

Don't be paranoid and think that everyone is against you. If someone criticises you, ask yourself whether there is a grain of truth in it without giving an immediate gut reaction.

Accept that sometimes life is tough: and that it's tough for everyone even if you can't see it. Most people have disappointments, make big mistakes, have tragedies happen, not just you. So it's not an excuse for you to react badly. Accept that there are other points of view as well as your own. You don't always have the right answers or they may not be right for everyone. Accept that others want the same things as you, such as being treated with respect, being treated justly, being valued; and not everyone can have them all of the time. Disappointment is a part of life.

Think of the things that have made you angry. Then put them in order with the minor situations first. Could you have looked upon these events differently? Could you have said, 'Well, it's done now. I can't change that so I may as well just move on'? or, 'Never mind. It could have been worse'? or, 'It's nothing that can't be put right.'

When things can't be put right, try to shake off the bad feelings. Say, 'Oh, well ...' or shrug it off with, 'That's life.'

Change the way you do things. If certain things make you angry and they can't be resolved because they keep happening, avoid the situation or ignore it.

Keep to the facts when addressing a problem. Do not

name call or throw aspersions on another person's character. State what you find unacceptable and then try to work with the other person to put it right. You must give the other person a chance to have his say and respect him enough to listen. By doing this you can save a relationship.

Throw yourself into something else when you find one avenue blocked to you. Think of it as a window opening when a door closes. This acts as a positive outlet for your disappointment or anger because it furthers your aims, albeit in a different way from what you had expected.

Learn relaxation techniques. Relaxation will help stop you from hyperventilating and relax your muscles generally so that your body is calmer during the day: you will be less likely to react violently when something goes wrong (see *Learn to relax* in Chapter 12). When your body feels very calm and relaxed, your mind will calm down too.

Delay the onset of your anger. By counting slowly to 10 or 20 either forwards or backwards, you can distract your mind sufficiently not to develop the full force of your anger immediately, buying you time to respond in a more rational way. Holding your breath briefly can also buy you time.

Slow down your mind. Slowing down your thoughts when you are in an anger-critical situation, gives you time to think about what you will say and do. This will also give the other person time to consider what she has just said or done.

Try to understand the other person's perspective by carefully listening to what he has to say. This will help you understand him and may show you that no offence is intended. If you don't understand what he's trying to say, ask him to explain.

Ask yourself if your thoughts are truly your thoughts or someone else's. Sometimes angry thoughts are put there by someone else, such as a parent who used the same words with you. If your thoughts are not your own, don't use them.

Stick to the issue and don't take the criticism personally. It doesn't help if you fight back with insults just because you don't like what you've heard. Discuss the matter brought up while ignoring any personal slights to keep the conversation focused. Deal with the personal slurs separately by asking for an apology or why the person called you such names and say how hurtful you found them.

Ask for time to think it over so that, when you do talk about what the other person has said, you'll be much more constructive, especially if you allow yourself to consider related things that others have said. If several similar comments from different people keep cropping up, you must give the other person the benefit of the doubt and take time to look at yourself objectively and consider whether there is truth in what's been said.

Leave the situation if you feel things are getting on top of you. This helps reduce your stress, helps you see things more objectively as you have removed yourself from the situation that was making you feel angry and upset, and will rejuvenate you so that you can return refreshed.

Get praise and positive feedback from others. To help motivate you in controlling your anger, tell the people close to you that you are going to try very hard to knock this one on the head. They will reward you with praise when you show you can handle your anger which will make you want to try even harder and so reap further rewards. Don't work alone on this.

If you can remember a time when you did control your anger, create an anchor for this experience (see *Anchors* in Chapter 9) so that you can recreate this feeling to help you deal with your anger in the future.

If you unleash your anger in circumstances where anyone would be hard put not to let rip, accept that something bad has happened to you. Personally acknowledge your feelings and tell others how you feel. Be kind to yourself and not over-critical at this time, as this will only make you feel worse about yourself and create more anger. However, violent behaviour is never acceptable.

If your anger is uncontrollable or ever present bubbling inside you and you cannot get through it, consider having counselling. You owe it to yourself and to those you deal with now and in the future. Some people, for example, are intensely jealous and feel they have a right to 'own' their partner, checking up if they are ten minutes late home and dictating who their partner can spend time with. If this describes your behaviour, you need to get help for your anger before it ruins your relationship.

Dealing with other people's anger

If someone is obviously angry, behave in a calm manner yourself: getting heated will only make matters worse. Don't raise your voice. Speak slowly, and ask him to listen to what you have to say – and make it clear you will listen to what he wants to say. Angry people do need to feel that they are being taken seriously and treated fairly. Don't start your sentences with 'You' as this can be seen as aggressive and accusing.

Roger was disgruntled because he felt he was being taken advantage of as his boss, Denyse, went home from work before he did. Roger said angrily, 'Why should you get paid more than me and get a posh company car when you don't know the meaning of work, coming in late and going home early?'

Denyse calmly replied, 'I can see how it looks to you but you don't know all the facts.'

'I bet I don't. You're probably here even less than I think.'

Denyse said, 'Will you let me reply to your comments? . . . Thank you. When you leave here, you leave all your work behind. I take mine home with me and often come in on weekends. Plus if things go wrong, it's on my head trouble falls, not yours. I have to take responsibility for it. If you think you could do just as well and don't mind putting in the hours I do, I suggest you apply for a management position.

'If you have a complaint about your own work schedule, I suggest you make an appointment to discuss it with me.' Denyse wanted to make clear she was the boss and although she was prepared to discuss Roger's working day, she wasn't going to do that while he was angry.

To show that you are listening to what the other person has to say, and are taking her concerns seriously, be quick to accept any blame that is yours and reject any blame that isn't yours, with reasons.

Patrick was late in picking up his young child from school. His wife screamed at him when he got home about his being irresponsible and told him about things that could have happened had the school not kept his son inside. She was also very upset for the stress he'd caused their son. Patrick said, 'Everything you've said is absolutely right. I am sorry. I forgot the time and then I had a phone call. I should have ignored it. And I'm sorry that my being late upset him. It won't happen again.'

If someone is not overtly aggressive and makes cutting comments about you, confront the comments and question their validity: 'Please give an example of when I've been heartless' – but don't make personal comments back. If the person can't substantiate what he said, ask for an apology: 'What you said was unkind and I didn't deserve to be called that. I'd like you to apologise.'

If you are in complete disagreement with someone, state your point of view and, if necessary, agree to disagree and leave it. If you want to explore the issue, try to meet the other person half way and show your willingness to do this by openly saying what you do agree with.

If the disagreement is over something that is yet to come rather than an opinion or something that has happened in the past, try to find middle ground that would be acceptable to both of you. It is counterproductive to try to 'win' – or have your way – at all costs. Finding a compromise will allow both you and the other person to gain in some way – it is better if you can both 'win'.

If the other person looks like he is out of control, there is no point in trying to get him to see things logically and calmly: it would be safer for you to leave.

11

PHOBIAS AND ANXIETY DISORDERS

Anxiety does not empty tomorrow of its sorrows, but only empties today of its strength.
Charles Spurgeon (1834–92)

This chapter gives an overview of some of the most common conditions relating to stress and anxiety. Although no specific advice is given for these anxiety disorders, advice on dealing with anxiety and panic in Chapter 12 will be of help as will the information on therapies in Chapters 14 and 15.

Phobias

A phobia is an extreme fear of something or a situation. Your response to the trigger that causes your fear is completely out of proportion to the danger it represents. People who suffer from phobias often suffer from panic attacks (see Chapter 12), particularly when they are in a situation from which they cannot escape. Phobias can be classed into three groups: specific phobias, agoraphobia and social phobia.

Specific phobias are fears of single things rather than

events or situations. These include: acrophobia (fear of heights); aerophobia (fear of flying); apiphobia (fear of bees); arachnophobia (fear of spiders); claustrophobia (fear of confined spaces); cynophobia (fear of dogs); gatophobia (fear of cats); musophobia (fear of mice); odontophobia (fear of dental work); ornithophobia (fear of birds) and trypanophobia (fear of injections).

Some specific phobias are easier to avoid than others. For example, if you have a fear of heights, unless you are housed or have to work in a high-rise building, you can avoid them, choosing not to work in a profession that requires you to climb ladders or work at heights. But if you have a phobia of bees, you may dread stepping out of your house or even opening a door or window during warmer weather.

Agoraphobia is one of the most common phobias and aspects of it are apparent in other anxiety disorders. It is a fear of open spaces (although not so common), of crowded places, of being alone, of having panicky feelings and being in situations where you feel that panicky feelings are likely.

A common fear is being in a place or situation where there is no escape, or no escape without considerable embarrassment – such as where it would be socially unacceptable to leave before the appropriate moment. If you suffer from agoraphobia your anxiety about having to stay mounts as you worry about needing the toilet, having diarrhoea, being sick, fainting, or having a panic attack.

Example situations include: being in a waiting room – you need to wait until you've had your appointment; queuing in a supermarket – you may wonder whether you can cope with being in the shop sufficiently long to pay for the goods; sitting in a dentist's or hairdresser's chair – you need to wait until the treatment or service is complete;

sitting in a middle row at the theatre or cinema – it is disruptive to the others in the row, and those seated behind, if you have to leave in the middle of a show or film; sitting in a restaurant – once the food is ordered, you feel obliged to remain until it is eaten and paid for; travelling on public transport – escape is not easy unless you get off before the intended stop but you may face a long walk or wait for the next bus or train, while your anxiety mounts (and you might need the loo).

Other potentially stressful situations for someone with agoraphobia include: being caught up in a traffic jam – there is no quick escape, and you may feel trapped; being in a car whilst driving yourself – you may suddenly feel a need to be back in the comfort and security of your home; being a passenger in someone else's car – you are dependent on the driver and may feel unable to relax, not knowing whether you will cope with the journey without needing to stop; being at home alone – you may fear being ill and being unable to cope alone or feel very anxious or insecure on your own.

You can feel so anxious in these situations that you suffer a panic attack. Many people who suffer from panic attacks can develop agoraphobia as they fear having a panic attack in situations where it would cause embarrassment or from where escape is not easy. Often they feel happier when they are out with a trusted person who can look after them if they feel panicky.

Agoraphobia most commonly starts in the late teens or early twenties; since it tends to worsen the longer it goes on, it is important to get professional help at an early stage. Therapy may involve cognitive behavioural therapy (CBT) and desensitisation (see Chapter 14).

Social phobia is an extremely common performance-related phobia where you fear making a fool of yourself in front of others or having your anxiety noticed – such as having a shaking hand when signing a document or sipping from a drink. It can either be general, where you fear all social occasions, or discrete (specific), where you worry about only one social situation such as public speaking.

People with general social phobia are sensitive to any form of rejection and may avoid social situations so that they cannot be criticised, marginalizing themselves from society. Worries they face include blushing – showing everyone they feel awkward; eating in public – fearing, for example, spilling their food or of not being able to eat; making conversation – fearing, for example, being thought stupid or others noticing a shaky voice; making a public speech – fearing, for example, how their voice carries, and whether it shakes or makes sense; writing – fearing, for example, that others notice their hand shaking.

Since, like agoraphobia, social phobia tends to worsen the longer it goes on, it is important to get professional help early on. Therapy may involve CBT and desensitisation (see Chapter 14).

Separation anxiety

Separation anxiety is anxiety you may have suffered as a child when separated from your parents beyond the expected years (including home-sickness in teenagers), but adults too can suffer from it. Prolonged or unresolved separation anxiety can develop into panic disorder (see below) and depression (see Chapter 13) in adults – you may not be able to function independently and fear every event you have to cope with alone, still needing the support of a parent; or you may have transferred your need of support to your partner.

Panic disorder

If you have panic disorder, you have repeated panic attacks with no apparent trigger, and you continually worry about when the next panic attack will come. Because the panic attacks are so frequent with no common theme to their trigger, you can easily develop other phobias, wanting to avoid places or situations where panic attacks occurred. But because they are so numerous, you may soon be avoiding all situations and may not even feel comfortable at home, as they can happen there too.

If your life is so restricted you do not want to go out, or to go out alone, you have agoraphobia too. It is essential you seek professional help early on, before agoraphobia develops, as it is then easier to treat.

Generalised anxiety disorder

If you suffer chronic anxiety, worrying far more than most people about everyday things and events, but do not suffer repeated panic attacks (and do not worry about having panic attacks), you are considered to have generalised anxiety disorder. You can feel constantly tense, anticipating disaster, worrying excessively about things that may never happen or may just worry about how you are going to get through the day. The constant anxiety that you feel can make you tense, jumpy and restless and can interfere with sleep, making it hard to fall asleep and to stay asleep.

Most sufferers can continue with their lives without avoiding situations – unlike with panic disorder. The onset is gradual and can start as early as childhood.

Eating disorders

Although eating disorders are not classified as anxiety disorders, they are common difficulties partly associated with stress and vulnerable personalities. People with eating disorders are likely to be emotionally sensitive, high achievers and perfectionists, yet will have very low self-esteem. They might fear becoming fat and be driven to become thin, relying on eating or refusing to eat in order to cope with emotional distress, stressful life events and body changes after puberty.

With all eating disorders, your emotions are tied up with the food that you eat. Problems with eating outlined below can overlap so that you do not suffer one eating disorder in isolation. Early professional help is recommended if you suffer from any eating disorder – they are potentially life-threatening and more difficult to treat the longer they go on. However, milder forms of bulimia nervosa can be self-helped without necessarily needing professional help.

If you are a compulsive eater, you may eat to comfort yourself, to make up for the things in life that you lack. Or you might compulsively eat when you are angry, worried or distressed. You might eat enormous quantities of food in a short space of time and afterwards feel so guilty and shamed that you induce vomiting. You may then try to go on a strict diet until the next time you lose control.

If you have bulimia nervosa, you may appear healthy and coping well with your life but in fact may have erratic eating patterns ranging from total starvation to eating thousands of calories at a time. After a 'binge' you might induce vomiting or take laxatives (to increase the speed of passage of food through the gut so that less is absorbed) and diuretics (to increase urination) and then return to a controlled diet until you lose control the next time.

If you have anorexia nervosa, you have not lost your appetite as the name suggests but have learned to deny it. You may feel out of control with the rest of your life and have only your eating left to control, restricting your food and liquid intake to very small quantities of calories. You probably wouldn't want to eat with anyone else either, wanting to do it in secret. You may often vigorously exercise to burn off calories and weigh yourself several times a day. However thin you are, you see yourself as fat and disgusting. When you lose control and binge, you are likely to purge yourself afterwards through vomiting or taking laxatives and diuretics, no matter how little has in fact been eaten.

Orthorexia nervosa is a relatively new type of eating disorder where the sufferer has an obsessional interest in healthy eating, losing perspective, ruling out non-organic, frozen, high-fat, sugar- and salt-containing foods and may be only eating raw and natural produce. If you have orthorexia, you may become as thin as someone with anorexia and be missing vital nutrients and can spend all day thinking about, planning and preparing food.

Obsessive compulsive disorder

Obsessive compulsive disorder (OCD) is a common disorder that is classified with anxiety disorders. It can start in childhood although its onset is more common in young adulthood. It is characterised by recurrent obsessional thoughts or compulsive acts.

Obsessional thoughts are repetitive ideas, images or impulses that are distressing because they are obscene, violent or senseless and they cannot be resisted. If you try to resist them, your anxiety mounts; when you give in to them you experience relief. Since obsessional thoughts take up so much of your day, you may be indecisive, finding it impossible to make even very simple decisions.

Compulsive acts – or rituals – are behaviours that you feel the need to repeat again and again, yet you get no pleasure from doing it, only relief from your anxiety. Performing these acts can take up many hours each day.

Examples of compulsive acts include repeated hand washing, counting things, hoarding, only walking on the lines on pavements, checking you have locked all the doors and windows, tidying a room so that the chair lines up with the window frame at a certain angle and the curtains are equidistant from the centre of the rail . . . The compulsion can also involve bringing to mind particular images – you may fear that if you don't do this, something terrible will happen.

Obsessive compulsive disorder can coexist with other conditions. If you suffer from OCD you may also have the following personality traits: chronic worrying, extreme feelings of guilt, a high sense of responsibility, perfectionism, hypersensitivity, a lack of confidence, feeling distressed by changes and a vivid imagination. If OCD is interfering with your life, you should seek professional help.

Some people have obsessive compulsive personality disorder without necessarily having obsessive compulsive disorder, although both can coexist. A person with obsessive compulsive personality disorder does not have obsessions and compulsions but does have a preoccupation with orderliness, perfectionism and control that has started from early adulthood.

Post traumatic stress disorder

Post traumatic stress disorder (PTSD) is the development of certain symptoms following exposure to an extreme traumatic stressor involving direct personal experience of an event that involves actual or threatened death or serious injury, or other physical threat; or witnessing these things.

Examples of traumatic events that may cause PTSD include: assault – physical or sexual; bombing or other terrorist act; burns, especially to your face; child abuse be it sexual, physical or fear of physical abuse, mental or emotional abuse; experience of war; lack of crowd control disasters such as being crushed in a football stadium or being hurt at a political demonstration; motor, rail, coach, car or aeroplane crashes; natural disasters such as earthquakes, volcano eruptions, fire and flooding; rape.

For a diagnosis of PTSD to be made, there needs to be a latency period from a few weeks to a few months (but rarely more than six months) before the symptoms develop. There are three main symptoms always present in PTSD. The first is hyper-arousal where you are on edge all the time, waiting for something else bad to happen or fearing a repeat situation. The second is intrusive memories and flashbacks that also include nightmares about the event. Similar situations might induce panic attacks even though the original danger is not present. The third symptom is emotional numbing where you feel unreal and detached from normal life and feelings.

You can also experience social isolation, cutting yourself off from others, unable to trust people. You might also feel angry and bitter at what has happened and guilty or ashamed of what you have done or failed to do. It is very common for sufferers of PTSD to suffer from depression and panic attacks. If you suffer from PTSD you should seek professional help.

12

ANXIETY AND PANIC

The time to relax is when you don't have time for it.
Sydney J. Harris (1917–86)

People who have low self-confidence and low self-esteem are more likely to be vulnerable to anxiety.

When you are highly stressed, your experiences may include: acting or feeling out of character, talking too loud or too fast; aggression, anxiety, hostility, irritability and impatience; biting nails or lips, drumming fingers, picking at skin, tapping feet; clenching your fists and jaw, grinding your teeth (dentists can make 'splints' to wear at night to protect teeth and gums), skin rashes (such as eczema and psoriasis); dependence on alcohol and drugs; depression, crying, difficulties with sleep, disturbing dreams, mood swings and forgetfulness; digestive problems such as abdominal pain and diarrhoea; fatigue, boredom, lack of concentration and apathy; feeling frustrated, helpless, hopeless, out of control, unsettled or restless; feeling hot and cold; hunched shoulders, muscular tension, headaches – including migraines – and muscle spasms and shakiness; impotence (in men) and lack of sex drive, and jumping at the slightest sound, palpitations, sweating, and nausea.

If the level of anxiety you experience stays high, or is

added to by another stressful event, you may feel panicky or even develop a panic attack. Constant stress or single stressful life events can lead to panic attacks in some people.

If you suffer from prolonged excessive stress, you may suffer either a physical breakdown (such as having angina, a heart attack, a stroke or a debilitating viral illness); or a mental breakdown (such as depression, being unable to function sufficiently to take care of yourself, episodes of uncontrolled screaming or weeping, self-mutilation or suicide). If any of the conditions mentioned below are interfering with your life or are distressing you to an uncomfortable degree, you must seek professional help: early intervention helps to prevent the condition worsening and spreading into other areas of your life.

Panic attacks

A panic attack is a short but intense feeling of fear that can last from a few minutes to several hours. The symptoms can be so severe that you feel as though you are dying, having a heart attack or are out of control. By understanding what causes panic, you are in a better position to overcome it.

Your first panic attack usually results from too high background stress that makes you over-breathe giving you unpleasant symptoms of hyperventilation.

Effects of hyperventilation

Hyperventilation causes an overload of oxygen, and too little carbon dioxide, in your blood. A low level of carbon dioxide makes your blood alkaline, which constricts your arteries reducing blood flow, especially to your brain. Since blood carries oxygen, constriction of arteries limits the amount of oxygen available to your brain.

The brain responds by telling your lungs to breathe even more, which exacerbates the problem. Unless you can override your breathing pattern with the thinking (frontal) part of your brain, hyperventilation and your fear over the symptoms can lead to a panic attack.

The effects of hyperventilation are: finding it hard to concentrate; blurred vision; a pounding heart – to increase your blood pressure to help blood get to your brain; feeling short of breath; feeling dizzy and faint; experiencing tingling sensations on your skin – in severe cases muscles can spasm, particularly in your face, hands and forearms; your hands and feet can become cold and numb – related to a reduced blood flow from constricted arteries; you might tremble or shake; your chest can feel tight or uncomfortable from muscles having to work hard at breathing and your chest may hurt; you may get palpitations, feel tense, anxious and weak; you may feel sick.

Escalating worry over your physical symptoms caused by hyperventilation kick-starts your 'fight or flight' mechanism, telling your lungs to breathe faster still, making your blood even more alkaline as it picks up more oxygen.

'Fight or flight'

Your body is not designed to deal with fear in a non-physical way – running from real danger, for example, uses up excess oxygen – so your increasing symptoms are not alleviated and you have a panic attack.

Many chemicals, including adrenaline and cortisol, get your body ready for 'fight or flight' when anxiety is high such as during a panic attack. Cortisol acts on the liver to make blood sugar to provide energy. Adrenaline has wide-ranging effects on your body.

Effects of adrenaline

It dilates, or widens, the airways in your lungs to increase their capacity and dilates the blood vessels that feed your muscles to increase the amount of oxygen and blood sugar available to them. It dilates your pupils to let in more light to make you more aware of your surroundings.

It constricts the blood vessels to your gut, kidney and liver to divert more blood to your muscles so digestion of food is halted. Your face becomes pale because the blood vessels in your skin are also constricted to divert blood to your muscles and to protect you from wounding; this can make you feel cold.

Your legs and knees feel weak because of the extra blood flowing into them not equalling the amount of blood leaving them, so it accumulates. If you were to start running or walking, the action of your muscles would help push blood back out of your legs.

It relaxes your gut to allow your diaphragm to press further into your abdomen to increase lung capacity and can relax your bladder and bowel muscles to give you diarrhoea and make you need to urinate so that your body is lighter for 'flight'.

It increases the strength and speed at which your heart beats to increase your blood pressure so that blood is pumped more quickly round your body to give plenty of blood sugar and oxygen to your muscles. This increase in blood pressure makes it less likely you will faint, despite fears you may have about fainting.

It tenses your muscles so that they are ready for action, which can make you feel tense all over, especially on the scalp, which makes your hair more erect. Although this is of no use to us, it is to cats as it makes them look bigger to their enemies. Tense muscles can give you neck ache, a headache and a feeling of having a tight band around your head and abdomen. Your throat muscles also become tense, making it hard to swallow.

It stops saliva production to conserve energy. This can cause an acid stomach – saliva helps to neutralise the acid in your stomach.

It increases sweating to get your body, which includes your palms, ready to cool on physical exertion and because of your increased metabolic rate – your body has to work very hard at the moment as it is on an emergency setting.

It acts on the part of your brain called the amygdala, which triggers an emotional response to tell you to be very afraid and avoid the stressor – unfortunately conditioning you to future avoidance behaviour.

It inhibits activity in the frontal part of the brain concerned with rational thought so you react instinctively to the situation, influenced by the amygdala.

The hippocampus in your brain stores information about your fearful situation – in this case, the panic attack – in its long-term memory so that you can respond quickly the next time something similar happens without needing the frontal part of your brain to consider it rationally as this takes longer.

It is such a powerful protective mechanism that you only need to have a panic attack once and you are conditioned for life to react in the same way when you are in a similar physical situation – such as being on a bus – or have similar physiological feelings – such as those created by fear. Whenever that memory is recalled in the hippocampus, the amygdala is triggered to give you the same emotional response of fear and avoidance, and immediately kick-starts the 'fight or flight' response in your body. This explains why people can have phobic reactions to non-dangerous situations.

Overcoming panic
The uncomfortable physical feelings of a panic attack can leave you feeling exhausted and drained, fearing a recurrence as the experience is so awful: you get the symptoms from 'fight or flight' as well as from hyperventilation. But not everyone has full-blown panic attacks and so their symptoms may be milder. Once you have had one panic attack, you are vulnerable to others.

The frontal part of your brain, concerned with rational thought, can override the unnecessary fear response involved in panic attacks. But it cannot erase the memory or change your reaction to it, although it can suppress it completely or partially. This would probably be fine if everything else in your life were going well and you felt strong and in control. But if you are overwhelmed by stress, such as by being under too much pressure or suffering illness, the memory can be triggered or heightened by these extra stressors. At weak times like these, the frontal part of your brain cannot dominate the amygdala and hippocampus and you have your next panic attack.

Coping with panic is not an easy task as the key to coping is acceptance and not fighting against your feelings of anxiety. Once you can recognise the first symptoms of anxiety that develop and learn to breathe deeply and slowly, using your diaphragm (see below), you can stop your anxiety escalating. If it does get out of control, let the feelings wash over you and wait for them to pass. This is the quickest way of averting a panic attack or reducing its length and severity.

Breathing techniques to reduce hyperventilation and panic
Anxiety symptoms can be relieved by breathing techniques, making panic less likely.

Breathe diaphragmatically: this can take a while to master. While you learn diaphragmatic breathing, put one hand on your tummy and another on your chest and note what happens to them. When you breathe in – through your nose, not your mouth – use your tummy to push your hand out. The hand on your chest should not move. This ensures that you are breathing deeply and not shallowly.

Try counting to 4 on the in-breath and another 4 on the out-breath to make sure you are breathing regularly and evenly. This makes you breathe out completely – without forcing the last bit of air out of your lungs – before you breathe in again. Breathing like this stops you hyperventilating. You should practise breathing like this whenever you can – it is the relaxed way to breathe. No one knows when you are practising this form of breathing so you can do it anywhere at any time.

The more you breathe diaphragmatically, the more you reduce the symptoms of anxiety and panic. Phobics Awareness suggest that if you have trouble with diaphragmatic breathing, kneel on the floor with your hands in front of you, assuming the position of a four-legged animal, because this tends to lock your chest in place, forcing the diaphragm to take over your breathing.

Count the number of breaths you take per minute. This should be around 12 per minute – one every 5 seconds – when you're at rest. If you are breathing more than this, check that you are breathing diaphragmatically and that your breaths are long and deep, taken in through your nose (it takes longer than breathing through your mouth so reduces the amount of oxygen you take in).

Monitor your breathing and your muscle tension: Put a small dab of correction fluid on your watch or watchstrap, where you will see it when you check the time. When you see this white dot, focus on your breathing and remind yourself to breathe diaphragmatically. At the same time, mentally scan your muscles (from your scalp to your toes) to see which are tense and consciously relax them. This reduces your underlying tension, bringing you to a higher level of relaxation at regular points throughout the day. When you have done this for some weeks, it will become second nature to you to relax and check that you are not becoming tense.

If there is a situation coming up where you know you will feel tense, try to enjoy it and live through it with floppy muscles and diaphragmatic breathing. This prepares you for dealing with panic-inducing situations, building your confidence to deal with more and more difficult situations.

Emergency relief from hyperventilation. When you feel dizzy and feel compelled to keep taking large gulping breaths, you need quickly to reduce the amount of oxygen entering your body. Breathe deeply into a *paper* bag, with the opening of the bag covering your nose and mouth, to re-breathe air that you have already exhaled; this brings up the concentration of carbon dioxide in your body, reducing the amount of oxygen.

You can carry a small paper bag with you in your pocket or handbag wherever you go – some shops still provide them – and retreat to your car or the loo to perform the paper bag trick in private.

Emergency relief from panic. When you are having panic symptoms as well as hyperventilating, perform this breathing cycle taught me by a yoga teacher – escape to where you can be alone:

a) Breathe out.
b) Close your mouth.
c) Pinch your nose with your right hand using your thumb and third finger.

d)   Place your first and second fingers together between your eyebrows.

e)   Release your thumb and inhale through your right nostril.

f)   Close your right nostril and hold your breath for 3 slow counts.

g)   Exhale through your left nostril, releasing your third finger.

h)   Breathe in through your left nostril and then close it. Hold your breath for 3 slow counts.

i)   Exhale through your right nostril, releasing your thumb.

j)   Inhale through the same nostril and then close it again. Hold your breath for 3 slow counts.

k)   Continue with this cycle until you feel calmer.

This exercise takes so much concentration that it can distract your mind, reducing your symptoms of anxiety. Once you have mastered the exercise, increase your level of concentration by counting out slowly to 3 or 4 on your out-breaths, 3 to 4 on your in-breaths and hold to 3 or 4 before you exhale.

When you have mastered this, try imagining the route your breath takes as you breathe. It comes in through your right nostril, past the back of your throat, down your windpipe into your lungs. When you hold your breath, imagine the oxygen from the air you just breathed in being exchanged for carbon dioxide from your blood. Then exhale, imagining the used air leaving your lungs and travelling up your windpipe, past the back of your throat and out through your left nostril.

If you can concentrate on doing all these things, your mind has no room for the thoughts that induced your panic and so your symptoms will gradually recede.

Distract yourself

If you can stop your mind concentrating on how bad your body feels, you can get some relief from the physical symptoms of anxiety and have a chance of regaining control, breaking the cycle of increasing fear that leads to a panic attack. Distracting yourself by the yoga technique described above is one way. Here are some other methods that you can use while in company.

At times of high anxiety, try closely examining a pen. Note its texture; how it feels – whether smooth or rough; how it looks – whether shiny or matt, the colour, whether it has any writing on it or a logo; how the switch works, the size and feel of it; what the nib looks like; how many sections there are to the pen, and so on.

Alternatively, count the number of bricks in the wall opposite you – if it has visible bricks; the number of colours you can see in the room; the number of right angles in the room or visually trace patterns on carpets or wallpaper.

Try mentally singing familiar songs such as nursery rhymes or counting back from 200 in 4s or anything else that you can occupy your conscious mind with.

Use your peripheral vision

A technique used in neuro-linguistic programming, explained by Andy Smith, NLP trainer based in Manchester, to calm your body is to do the following:

Find a point on the wall that is straight in front of you and slightly above your eye level and stare at it in soft focus. Let your field of vision gradually broaden out, without moving your eyes, until you are aware of what you can see at the very edge of your vision – both sides at once. At the same time let your jaw muscles relax, and breathe easily. Be aware of what is happening behind you too to get 360° awareness. This activates the parasympathetic nervous system which calms your body down. It also calms your internal dialogue and slows your heartbeat. You may notice your hands gradually become warm. After staying in this relaxed state for a while, gradually come back to normal waking consciousness by narrowing your vision.

Learn to relax

Buy a relaxation recording to help you relax and notice what your body feels like when it is in a deep state of relaxation. You can use it before stressful situations or to help you fall into a relaxed and refreshing sleep. Some people use relaxation recordings two or three times a day when their stress levels are generally too high because they feel they have too much to cope with and feel close to 'cracking up'.

A quick way of relaxing is to tense all your muscles, including facial muscles, as tight as you can and hold for three seconds. Then relax them and breathe out, imagining hot water trickling down you at the same time or imagining that you are as floppy as a rag doll. Combining this with diaphragmatic breathing (see above) makes this a powerful relief to tension that builds up through the day. Repeat this whenever you are conscious of your tension building up.

For a longer relaxation session try this:

1.   Lie on your bed in a dark and quiet room.
2.   Lie on your back with your arms by your sides, your fingers gently curled, and your legs slightly apart.
3.   Throughout breathe diaphragmatically and in turn tense and release different muscle groups. Start by tightly screwing up your face. Hold for 3 long counts

and then release, feeling the tension leave your face. Consciously note what it feels like to be relaxed. Do this after every time you relax a muscle group.

4. Tense your neck and shoulders; hold and relax.

5. Tense one arm and hand, then the other, each time holding and then relaxing.

6. Tense your chest muscles; hold and relax.

7. Tense your abdomen and buttocks, pulling your tummy in and clenching your buttocks. Hold and relax.

8. Tense your right leg and foot (you can hold your leg a few centimetres up from the bed), hold and relax. Repeat with the left leg and foot.

9. Tense your entire body: concentrate on getting every possible muscle tensed. Hold and relax.

10. Concentrate on how your body feels.

11. Keep scanning your body to check that each muscle group is relaxed and, before you leave that group to scan the next, tell yourself how floppy the muscles are and how you feel your face, arm, leg, etc., melting into the bed. Let go all your tension.

12. After 20 minutes or so if it is the daytime, slowly come out of your relaxed state and say to yourself 'Wide awake and fully alert' – or, if it's at bedtime, just let yourself fall asleep.

13

CHRONIC LOW MOOD AND MILD CLINICAL DEPRESSION

Show me a thoroughly satisfied man and I will show you a failure.
Thomas A. Edison (1847–1931)

The suggestions in this chapter are to help change your life around, to see things differently. There is no intention of suggesting that you should 'pull yourself together' but it is down-to-earth advice that may help get you out of the rut/s you are in, to help dispel the worst of your chronic low mood and mild clinical depression.

Depression is a serious illness that carries the real risk of suicide. If you think you might harm yourself, you must see your doctor to get appropriate help. Early treatment can help prevent the condition worsening and lessen the likelihood of having a long-term problem.

Depression

Depression is a continued state of deep unhappiness that is experienced over a long period. Sometimes the depression is 'reactive' in that it follows a distressing life event such as bereavement or divorce. But sometimes there is no apparent reason for it.

Common symptoms of depression include: being unable to concentrate or remember things; being unable to express yourself effectively; being unable to smile; being unable to talk naturally to others; eating more or less than usual; feeling detached from others and not being able to experience loving feelings others have towards you, and of loving feelings you have towards others; feeling isolated and alone, feeling no one understands you; feeling sad and hopeless, despairing of anything ever changing; feeling tired and lethargic; feeling useless and worthless; having bursts of anger or impatience, having increased anxiety; insomnia or excessive sleeping; lack of drive and motivation, lack of sex drive; losing interest in things you previously liked; not washing as often as you should and not taking care of yourself; overworking to dull your mind; suffering from multiple minor aliments; tearfulness and thinking about death and suicide.

Depression can be triggered by certain illnesses; by hormonal disorders/imbalances such as those caused by birth control pills and by hormone replacement therapy; by disturbing and/or traumatic events or changes in life; by tension or stress; by chemical imbalances in the brain; by thyroid disorders; by poor diet and lack of exercise, and by premenstrual and postnatal effects.

Dysthymia
Chronic low mood, known as dysthymia, is an ever-present low-level depression that has gone on for many years, possibly as the result of an unhappy childhood or a series of events not going your way, gradually wearing down your internal resources. Low mood that has been with you for a long time is not just magically going to

disappear; use the advice in this chapter to help push back the worst of it so that it only becomes a problem when something else in your life goes wrong.

For a diagnosis of dysthymia to be made, you will need to have been suffering from a low mood for most of the time for most days for at least two years – without a major depressive episode – causing problems for you socially and at work, and you must have at least two of the following symptoms: overeating or loss in appetite, sleeping more or less than is usual, feeling tired all the time, finding it hard to concentrate or make decisions, having low self-esteem and having feelings of hopelessness – and these symptoms aren't attributable to drugs or medication or another diagnosable medical condition.

Seasonal affective disorder

Seasonal affective disorder is another common form of depression where sufferers feel depressed during the winter months because of a lack of sunlight reaching their brain. If you suffer from this, you may benefit from light therapy where you are exposed to light from specially-made lamps or you may benefit from a holiday in the sun or from spending more time outdoors.

Clinical depression

Clinical depression may be diagnosed if you have had five or more of the symptoms described below for at least two weeks – and they are severe enough to affect your social and working life – and they can't be accounted for by bereavement or another disturbing or traumatic event, the effects of a drug or medication, or a medical condition.

Symptoms of clinical depression are: having a persistent low mood or being anxious most of the day, most days; having too little or too much sleep most days;

having a loss in appetite and weight loss, or a gain in appetite and weight gain – the weight changes need to be more than 5 per cent of your body weight per month; having difficulty concentrating, remembering or making decisions; restlessness or slowing down of your body movements to the extent that it is noticeable by other people; having significant or complete reduction in interest in things you previously enjoyed, most days; having persistent physical symptoms that don't respond to treatment such as headaches and back ache; fatigue or loss of energy most days; feeling guilty, hopeless or worthless; thinking about death and suicide.

Seeing things in perspective

People with depression largely see themselves, their future and their everyday experiences, in a negative light. If you can relate to this, ask yourself how a friend or a stranger would see your life. Consider how you would see someone else's life if he told you the same things you could tell him. Would it be the catastrophe you are picturing for yourself? This will help you to see your problems objectively.

Another exercise that is useful in getting things into perspective is to note any labels you apply to yourself. For example, if you think you are a useless person, draw a horizontal line that represents the level of usefulness any person could have, the far right representing complete usefulness and the far left representing extreme uselessness. Mark a cross on the line where you think you lie in your level of usefulness. Then ask yourself what the most useless person in the world would be like. In the light of this, check whether you have placed yourself on the correct position of the line: you will probably find that you need to move yourself closer to the useful end. If this does not happen, ask a close friend to judge where you should be on the line after explaining what the exercise is about. Ask the friend why he placed you at that point.

Unhelpful thinking

People with depression have thought patterns that are negative and damaging to themselves in that they help to perpetuate their depression; therapists call these negative automatic thoughts or NATs. If you can identify unhelpful thought patterns and see things instead as they really are, you will help to push back your low mood (this is covered more thoroughly in *Skewed thoughts* in Chapter 14).

Also, try to change the way you think about your past. For example, if you had a very unhappy childhood and believe that, because of this, you will never be happy, think again. Although you cannot change what happened in the past, you can try to change the way you think about it. What has your past done to you as a person? You are probably more understanding of others, easier to talk to, less judgmental, more sensitive in your dealings with others – and know not to make similar mistakes with your own children, having been alerted to those pitfalls.

Unhelpful behaviours

There are certain behaviours people with depression exhibit that actually perpetuate their low mood. You need to identify behaviour that feeds your depression and work at ways to change it; this will help to correct your NATs so that you see the world and react to it as it really is.

The things mentioned below may be extremely hard for you to do when in a low mood state. But if you don't do them, you are helping to perpetuate your depression. Think of these things as your personal mountains to climb and praise yourself when you achieve them: every time.

Don't spend all day in bed – you will become unfit and so

feel less well and so will be more likely to stay depressed, and you won't experience a sense of achievement which will also make you feel depressed.

Take exercise – or you won't relieve your stress and won't benefit from increasing the amount of endorphins your body produces. (These are chemicals that are similar to morphine. They are natural painkillers and lighten your mood.)

Eat properly and don't go for long periods without eating as it will make you feel worse. Regular meals and snacks aimed at keeping your blood sugar levels steady will help how you feel. Try to eat a sensible breakfast each morning and eat a balanced diet, taking care that you have a good mix of all the nutrients your body needs.

Don't over-eat – it will only serve to make you feel bloated and disgusted with yourself and will not help your depression. You also risk getting more depressed if you gain weight when you are already over-weight.

Have a routine – without it your day lacks purpose. Decide on a sensible routine and stick to it: there can be comfort in routine and it can motivate you to do things even when you don't feel like it.

Have some interests – or your day won't contain rewarding experiences. Try to remember what your previous interests were if you have become inactive and rekindle them. Even going through the motions will be helpful as it will keep you occupied and you will have less time to think negatively. Make plans for each day and stick to them. You will feel happier during the day and more fulfilled by the end of each day. Don't be too ambitious: stick to what you're familiar with and know you will enjoy. Then reward yourself for having done it. (See *Rewarding yourself* in Chapter 3.)

Don't avoid social contact – it will help your depression

(see *Creating social security* in Chapter 9). If you don't feel up to pretending to be cheerful, perhaps you could arrange to do something with another person so that you're active rather than relying on conversation alone to pass the time. This makes it easier the next time you see that person as you've recently had a shared experience.

Relating to others

Increase your personal awareness of how you relate to others – you may be lowering your mood because you don't have great intercommunication skills and so block other people from warming to you.

For example, you might regard other people from your own perspective only and not listen to what they have to say or you might have a clear picture of what is right and wrong and not accept that there can be grey in-between areas. Or you might be subjective – applying your own rules and judgments to people. You might also select evidence to support your opinions, discarding evidence that doesn't – and accept any prejudices you might have, or confirm your view of people by goading them into action that will fulfil your prejudiced image of them.

Try to see things from other people's viewpoints; try to understand the whole picture and accept that things can be partly right and partly wrong; look at all the evidence objectively and don't be in a hurry to draw conclusions; avoid prejudices; listen to other people and avoid conflict.

Someone I once knew had very few friends and he seemed proud of the fact that he was so selective. He had mentally built an obstacle course through which people had to negotiate their way. If they were unsuccessful, he didn't make overtures of friendship towards them. At the first sign of a break in trust, they were discarded forever without trying to understand why the thing had happened or whether it had been a misunderstanding.

If you deliberately make life hard for others, don't let them get near you and don't make the effort of being open to new relationships, you are not likely to have very rewarding ones yourself which add to your depression. And if you have particular negative traits that you know you should address, such as a problem with anger, you need to overcome them so that you don't damage any more relationships.

Dealing with a personal crisis

Have a working list – one that you add to from time to time as ideas come to you – of helpful things and unhelpful things in your life regarding your mood and how you feel about yourself (see *Weeding your garden* in Chapter 9). Use this list when you are in a crisis to remind you of what things to limit or avoid and what things to increase to help you feel better.

Reach out to people you know will be helpful to you. Be prepared to tell them how you feel.

Avoid making any major decisions at this time as they are not likely to be made logically.

Don't take on too much as this will put you at greater risk of depression. Do less rather than more. Now is a time to pull in your boundaries instead of expanding them. (Liken this to erecting a windbreak for your hot air balloon, mentioned in Chapter 9.)

Don't put yourself in a position where something will be expected of you: if you are feeling emotionally empty and very low, you may feel that you simply do not have anything left to give.

Be extra kind to yourself. Make time to be alone and be peaceful and to do things you enjoy. Give yourself treats. This will help keep you emotionally centred or balanced.

Be patient: accept that it takes time for you to recover and feel emotionally energised.

Don't allow the bad things that happen to you to have a lasting effect. They do not have the right to overtake, and ruin, your life.

Try to fill yourself with self-love and allow small good things that happen to you to grow in significance to out-weigh the bad things.

Re-think your current obligations. Are there some things you could get shot of – or share them with someone else? If so, work out how best to do this; if you don't feel you can, can you change the way you view these obligations?

Be aware of the need to ask for practical help as well as emotional. To help you judge what you could ask, imagine what you would be willing to do for that person if asked and base your request on that.

14

COGNITIVE BEHAVIOURAL THERAPY

Reason can in general do more than blind force.
Gaius Cornelius Gallus (70–26 BC)

Cognitive behavioural therapy (CBT) is a form of psycho-therapy that combines cognitive and behavioural techniques to have a more beneficial effect than using one set of techniques in isolation. Cognitive techniques and behavioural techniques (see below) are used to relieve a person's symptoms by changing skewed thoughts, assumptions or beliefs about the world, and unhelpful behaviours; they can be extremely useful in self-help.

The way you feel about something cannot be changed directly. For example, you can't simply say to yourself, 'I don't like giving speeches. From now on I will like them and even enjoy them' and expect this to work. Indirect methods have to be used which are a combination of changing the way you think (cognitive therapy) and changing the way you behave (behavioural therapy). Most cognitive therapy includes elements of behavioural therapy, and most behavioural therapy includes elements of cognitive therapy, so the two are closely linked.

It is commonly known that Pavlov conditioned his dogs to salivate at the sound of a bell. But he also showed that once his dogs were conditioned to salivate, if food was not always produced at the sounding of the bell the dogs stopped salivating. They had been reconditioned to behave as they had before, without salivating at the sound of a bell. You can also recondition yourself to think and feel differently, which is what CBT is about.

Among the many difficulties that can be treated by CBT are depression, anxiety, anger, shame, eating disorders, family and marital difficulties and addictions.

Cognitive techniques

The way you feel about certain thoughts and certain things that have happened to you and about how you view your world, or how you think others see you, affects you emotionally. These emotions can affect the way your body feels – by producing different chemical secretions and bodily reactions – and so you change your behaviour, to one of avoidance, for example, because of it.

As you react to how your body feels, you can become conditioned in an unhelpful way. For example, if you dread having to make a speech at a formal event such as a wedding, your thoughts will affect your emotions and so your body will react producing chemicals that stress you and make you feel unwell. Because you feel unwell, you will start to worry about feeling ill and even being ill during your speech. You can thus become conditioned to thinking that giving speeches makes you unwell so you avoid them. This is obviously nonsense, as the act of speaking cannot make you ill: it is your thoughts that accompany the process of having to prepare and later give a speech that makes you ill.

Skewed thoughts

Although unhelpful thinking was mentioned in Chapter 13, it is appropriate to revisit the subject, since cognitive therapy involves identifying and dealing with skewed thoughts and distorted views about yourself and the world around you. Common distortions in thinking include the following.

You might label yourself in a negative way such as being stupid, boring or worthless. And if, for example, someone is rude to you, you might accept this event as reinforcing the message you have given yourself about being worthless without seeing it in perspective: that it is what one person thinks of you at this moment, not what everyone thinks of you all the time.

Had you been thinking logically, you might have wondered why this person was rude. There are many possibilities: she could have had a bad day and has taken it out on you; you may have irritated her because she was in a bad mood and was ready to snap at anyone; she might be jealous of you; she could be repeating what someone had said to her earlier in the day; you may have done something genuinely to upset her – you could ask her what it is and clear up the misunderstanding, apologising if appropriate.

You might over-generalise. For example, you might think, 'I was turned down at the interview so I can't be employable.' One occasion of being turned down does not mean you are unemployable. You cannot judge your entire self on one event alone. If you have been turned down regularly then there is a problem with your performance – interview techniques can be learned – or you are going for the wrong jobs or you need to make yourself a more marketable proposition by improving your people skills, gaining related work experience, or by going on a course.

You might think in 'all or nothing' terms. You might think that just because something didn't go so well, it was a complete disaster. Or you might think of people as being good or bad but not recognise the middle view of there being good and bad in everyone. More balanced outlooks help to make you feel better.

You might take comments and actions personally when they may not have been directed at anyone in particular. For example, if someone says to a crowd of you, 'I'm leaving, it's boring here' you might think he is leaving because he considers you boring. If you are at a party and you see a complete stranger frowning at you, you may believe he doesn't like you or that he is angry with you, despite you never having met him before. Perhaps he just has a headache.

You might also take the blame for something that was not your fault. For example, if someone is irritable with you, you might think, 'I must have done something to upset him.' Does that make sense? Question your reasoning.

You might catastrophise – thinking what has happened as being far worse than it actually is. For example, you may have clumsily handled a problem your child has and then believe that you are the worst dad ever. Or you might think that one argument with your partner means the relationship is over. Both these things can be repaired; you need to talk about the situation calmly with the people involved and apologise if appropriate.

You might believe you are inadequate and worthless because that is how you feel.

You might discount positive comments said about you as untrue, passing them off by thinking, 'Well, if she knew me she wouldn't be so praising' or, 'It's something anyone could have done.'

You might foretell things in a negative way which help to

fulfil self-limiting beliefs. For example, you might think, 'There is no point in trying as I'm bound to fail' or, 'I can't do that so there's no point in trying' or, 'I know what the answer will be, so I won't ask.' Attitudes like this bring you failure. If you were really fired up and motivated about something, you'd keep going at it until you reached your goal, adapting yourself as necessary to increase your chances of success.

You may believe that, because you are like you are now, you'll never be able to change. This is a defeatist attitude that will not reap rewards of moving forwards.

You might think everything would be fine if only you were something else such as beautiful or clever or slimmer or less skinny. Plenty of people who are, for example, over-weight have successful careers and relationships. It is not so much your body size that prevents you from becoming fulfilled and successful but your thoughts and personality, which you can work on. If you feel very distressed about your body size, ask your doctor to refer you to a specialist and learn how to eat sensibly; if you are comfort eating, you need to address the reasons why.

Other things to ask yourself are: would other people view the situation in the same way? Would you view it differently if you felt confident? What are the worst and best things that could happen? Decide on a more realistic outcome – somewhere between these two answers. How would you view the situation if a friend were telling you about what had happened to him? Very often, you would be kinder and more forgiving of another person than you would be of yourself.

Underlying beliefs
When you get to know someone you make judgments about him on: what you know of him; what you have

observed; what others say of him; how you feel about him; what you can remember of him; what you know of others like him; what has happened to you in the past; how he behaves towards you; what you've heard him say of you; what others tell you what he's said of you, etc.

These give you underlying beliefs about him, which may be fairly accurate – but it is easier to be objective when considering someone else. When considering yourself, you are unconsciously subjective, particularly if you have low self-esteem, as you will tend towards negativity and over-critical judgments, taking your already half-formed beliefs about yourself and confirming them.

Assumptions about the world around you are the rules you have set yourself by which you live. For example, if you have been betrayed in a relationship you might have the belief that it is best not to trust anyone; or that you mustn't tell someone about a very private matter as she won't keep it secret. You might believe that others find you boring or that no one in his right mind would want to talk to you so you make no attempt to talk to him.

Re-look at your expectations and life rules to identify over-high expectations of yourself that often make you fail because you cannot fulfil them. These high personal expectations are due to underlying beliefs about how others view you and what you think they expect of you – you are worried about losing good opinion or respect.

For example, if you have the expectation, 'I must be liked by everyone to be a success' it is not hard to see that this is unrealistic – you are thinking in 'all or nothing' terms. How many people do you know who are genuinely liked by everyone? I don't know of any. Thinking of all the personalities and different values and habits people have, it would be impossible for any one person to be liked by everyone else. A more helpful and more realistic view would be, 'I must work hard at having a core of friends with whom I am very close and accept that I can't be friends with everyone.'

If you have the expectation that, 'To be any good, I must pass all my exams first time' then you are setting a hard task for yourself. Do you know anyone who has been successful and not passed exams first time? Many people have got to great heights without having much of an academic background. No one thinks less of them for it. It's obviously not the passing of exams that stops people from succeeding; it's their attitude and how they use their personal resources and how well motivated they are. A more realistic and helpful view would be, 'It's where you get to that counts, not how quickly. And exams can be retaken.'

Having a life rule of, 'There is no point trying to make friends with the people I work with – they don't like me' isn't helpful. It gives you an excuse not to try to make friends with the people you work with. All relationships have to be worked at and you probably haven't made the effort before or in an inappropriate way.

If you want to have a friendly atmosphere at work and be included in social events, this attitude will not help you get it. Try to be friendly towards everyone you work with and see what happens. Some people will become friends and others won't. But at least you'd have tried. Look at everyone at work afresh and work out the things you like about each of them, rather than concentrating on why you don't like any of them, which was what you were probably doing before. Remind yourself of their positive points when you deal with them and perhaps even tell them what they are. Change your life rule to, 'I'll be more positive in my dealings with other people in future and will be the first to offer a hand of friendship.'

Another unhelpful life rule is, 'Even though I dislike my job, I mustn't change it as it would be seen as failure if I admitted I couldn't hack it.' This way of thinking isn't helpful because you are forcing yourself to stay in a situation that makes you miserable for a rule that no one else will appreciate or have any benefit from.

Your life rules should be made to look after you and get the best for you. This one is damaging. Leave or take your problems to your boss or Human Resources Department. If you make a logical list of the problems and suggest solutions to show that you are realistic in your requests and not just complaining for the sake of it, he may consider your needs seriously. You could change your life rule to, 'I should stick out any new job for a while so that I get a good feel for it. But if it makes me unhappy in the long term I should do something about it. That takes more courage than staying put or not trying to change things.'

Other unhelpful life rules include: My house must always be clean and tidy in case someone calls; I must always look my best; I should never show my feelings as that makes me feel vulnerable.

Other thoughts to check include: Am I writing myself, or someone else, off because of one bad experience? Am I concentrating too much on my weaknesses and ignoring my strengths? Am I taking the blame for something that wasn't my fault? Am I expecting myself to be perfect? Am I assuming I am powerless to change whatever is happening?

Behavioural techniques

The way you behave can affect you emotionally. When you are reconditioned to behave differently, your future behaviour reinforces this reconditioning because you realise that now the bad things don't happen to you or not in the same way. By repeating experiences again and again you eventually accept the new conditioning above the false unhelpful one.

Since people more readily adopt behaviour that is rewarded you need to have goals and rewards to motivate you – but this does not work the opposite way: if you don't manage something, don't beat yourself up over it. Think up ways to reward yourself for every tiny step you take in the right direction – from a mental pat on the back to a major personal celebration.

Skewed behaviour
Skewed behaviour is behaviour you have learnt from false conditioning such as by perceiving yourself to fail at something and so never wanting to repeat the experience. For example, if you suffer from social phobia and avoid all social invitations to dinner or to parties because you know that if you go you will feel unwell, you avoid going and so feel fine. Your behaviour has taught you not to do things that cause you anxiety which might give you temporary relief but you will feel left out and inadequate as a consequence.

When you avoid anything because of feeling anxious, you give up trying to overcome the difficulties and they become insurmountable. So the way you feel, and your avoidance behaviour because of it, affects your thinking: you have convinced yourself you are better off avoiding stressful situations, without regard as to whether it is logical to do so.

By changing your behaviour you can reinforce your re-aligned thoughts from cognitive therapy, making you feel better still. For example, if you dread going to work because you think no one likes you, re-align this thought to, 'They probably don't look pleased to see me because I don't look pleased to see them.' Behave as though you are genuinely pleased to see someone by smiling at her and saying hello in a cheery way. How does she respond? Probably similarly but if you've been surly with her for years she may initially distrust your sudden charm. So you need to do this on a regular basis. Can you now say that she doesn't like you? Now you know that if you make your behaviour towards others more rewarding, you will get more warmth back. Changing your behaviour in this way will help reinforce your thinking to the realistic view rather than the distorted one.

You can also change the way you feel by using behaviour that makes others change theirs. In the above example, you had done this in an indirect way by smiling at someone and getting a smile back. Changing someone else's behaviour in a direct way can be by saying no to him (see Chapter 5) so that he finally stops taking advantage of you; or by standing up for one of your rights (see Chapter 4). Doing this will make you feel more in control, confident and powerful: you are in charge of your own life.

Desensitisation is another way of re-aligning skewed behaviour: repeating an experience so often that it loses its terrors. For example, if you understand that it's your thoughts that make you feel ill when you have to give a speech, you can gradually teach yourself that this belief is true by progressively increasing your ability to speak publicly. You might, for example, decide to give a toast to a friend at dinner or to ask for silence in the office at work to make an announcement and so gradually build up to speaking in front of a larger audience (also see *Self-improvement goals* in Chapter 8).

Flooding is desensitisation by being exposed to the full measure of your fear. For example, if you are afraid of spiders and someone makes you hold a spider for half an hour, by the end of it you may have lost your fear: but you would also have had a very unpleasant time. Gradual desensitisation is easier to cope with.

Relaxation techniques can also help re-align skewed behaviour. If you can monitor your bodily reactions during the event and consciously get your body to relax tense muscles, prevent hyperventilation and panic attacks, you will cope much better (see Chapter 12). This will help change the way you think about the event because you will feel less stressed when doing it – and you might even enjoy it!

You can also practise relaxation techniques at home and use them to desensitise yourself to an event by imagining yourself in the situation while you are in a deep state of relaxation. Here you get used to doing the thing but without the uncomfortable feelings that accompany it in real life. This will then help when you have to do the thing in reality.

Modelling is a behavioural change that has nothing to do with *re*conditioning, as in the above examples. For example, if you are shy and socially anxious you can observe others' social behaviour and reproduce it in a way to suit your personality. You have not had to undo false learning as you are learning it for the first time.

Watch how others behave when in social situations and reproduce this behaviour in your own special way. Watch other 'successful' people to see how they achieve their goals. How do they behave socially? How do they behave when talking over the telephone? How do they manage their children? How do they deal with arguments with their spouse? How do they manage work conflicts? There is much you can learn and use to help yourself.

CBT and panic attacks

To understand that the symptoms people have from panic attacks are purely from the way they breathe, therapists may ask their clients to perform a behavioural experiment by deliberately over-breathing for two minutes. (This is not safe for people with certain medical conditions including epilepsy, heart and lung problems and pregnancy.)

Clients will experience unpleasant symptoms (described in Chapter 12) that are similar to those experienced in a panic attack and so will understand that nothing catastrophic is happening, but the normal effects of too much oxygen. This can help them deal with their panic on a more practical level, rather than thinking that dealing with it is beyond them.

If their panic thoughts are re-aligned to more realistic phrases, they are further helped. The clients can note what negative automatic thoughts they have during the over-breathing experiment and work with their therapists in challenging them, which is a cognitive technique.

The therapists would then move on to behavioural techniques and teach their clients how to breathe to prevent hyperventilation (described in Chapter 12) and ask them to practise it until it becomes second nature so that they can consciously use this way of breathing in stressful situations where there is a tendency to hyperventilate. The therapists would also teach relaxation techniques. The clients thus become empowered to prevent panic attacks.

Another useful technique is using coping statements to help you, such as, 'I have been able to do this in the past and will again' and, 'It doesn't matter if it doesn't work out; at least I'd have tried' and, 'Although feeling this anxious is unpleasant, I know it will pass.'

15

OTHER THERAPIES

Although the world is full of suffering, it is full also of the overcoming of it.
Helen Keller (1880–1968)

The therapies mentioned below are widely practised in the UK. Although described separately, in practice therapists can use techniques and approaches from therapies other than the one they may be using in the main. Eclectic therapy is when the therapist can tailor the therapy to suit the client, having expertise in a number of different therapeutic techniques from more than one therapy approach.

Although these therapies are only described very briefly, knowledge of the techniques used can show you the direction to take in self-help and demystify what goes on in a therapist's room; many people are anxious about seeking therapy and worry about the form it will take.

Psychodynamic therapy

Psychodynamic therapy (also called psychoanalysis or psychoanalytic psychotherapy) is a general name for therapeutic methods of bringing your unconscious – or subconscious – feelings, that may have been too painful to acknowledge, to consciousness so that you can experience and understand them.

Psychodynamic therapy helps you deal with, for example, emotional pain, depression, anxiety and difficulties with relationships and setting goals. It helps you to understand better how your mind works – known as gaining insight – to help you make changes and find solutions to your problems. This type of therapy can take a long time – a year or more – as it explores your past, present and personality in detail.

Two techniques that the therapist uses to uncover hidden or forgotten memories are free association – talking to the therapist about anything that comes to mind without consideration, allowing your unconscious to direct you to what is important to you, revealing needs and memories of which you are unaware – and dream interpretation – so that the therapist can look at patterns and timing of your dreams in relation to what's going on in your life.

In this type of therapy the therapist does not offer advice or tell you what to do, but allows you to explore your feelings in a safe environment without fear of judgment from the therapist.

Focal psychodynamic therapy is a shorter version of psychoanalysis where the therapy is more focused such as when addressing a specific problem like a phobia.

Solution focused brief therapy

Solution focused brief therapy, SFBT (also known as solution oriented brief therapy) takes up as few sessions as possible and does not dwell much on your past, unlike psychodynamic therapy, as it works on the assumption that clients can be helped without needing to understand fully the reasons for their difficulties. Therapists seek to find solutions to difficulties that exist in the present and

SFBT is very much goal-oriented with you (and possibly your family – see *Systemic family therapy* on page 168) and the therapist working together to find solutions.

The solutions and goals are your solutions and goals and not the therapist's: you work collaboratively with the therapist to achieve what you want to achieve – and the therapist will help you identify what it is that you want. Then the therapist will help you find the most direct route to get you there, using knowledge from what you have said about what is already working at tackling the difficulty. The therapist may ask questions like, 'How will you know this is helping you?' to help clarify your goals and, 'How will you know you no longer need help?' to help determine when the end of the therapy has been reached. Although you may not have got to where you want to be when therapy ends, you will know by this time that you are able to achieve it and what you have to do.

One of the core beliefs of SFBT is that you have all the resources you need at your disposal to solve your problems. It focuses on your strengths and abilities rather than on your weaknesses, looking at times, for example, when you either don't currently have the difficulty, or didn't have the difficulty in the past, to discover what the difference is – looking for exceptions to the difficulty – to supply a solution. Understanding how these times brought about an absence of the difficulty helps you recreate the things that do not allow the difficulty to exist in the future. If you cannot remember an exception to your difficulty – either when the difficulty wasn't there or it impinged on you less – the therapist may ask you to try doing something in a different way to see what will happen in the hope that this might find a solution.

You may be asked to scale your difficulty by giving it a number between 0 and 10 (where 10 is the most positive score, having a complete absence of the problem; and 0 is the most negative score, being the worst possible scenario related to the problem). The therapist can then ask why you have rated your difficulty at that number and what things would have to be like for you to give your score another point in the positive direction. Should your scale increase between sessions it can help identify what you have done differently to help your difficulty (which can help you know what you have to do to improve it further) and how this change has affected your life and the life of those around you. The therapist will encourage you to build on small successes and to identify things that don't work or make the difficulty worse.

You may also be asked questions like, 'What are you doing that helps you cope with your difficulty?' or, 'What are you doing that stops your difficulty from worsening?' or, 'How have you approached problems in the past?' to help find your strengths. This helps you to see yourself in a new light, recognising the power in you to make a change.

In looking for your strengths, and how you deal with your difficulty, the therapist may compliment you on what you have achieved or the qualities you have displayed – something you may not do yourself as you may take these things for granted and concentrate only on what is bad in your life. The therapist's compliments will help you see yourself more objectively and enable you to recognise the talents you have and make use of them.

SFBT also looks into what life would be like for you if you no longer had the difficulty (therapists call this the 'miracle question'), to help you reach your goal and concentrate on what you do want. (It might be clear to you what you *don't* want, but it is much more helpful to identify what you *do* want.)

You might be asked, 'If a miracle happens in the night

and you wake up tomorrow without your problem, how would you know it was no longer there?' You may be asked to describe what a whole day would be like for you without your problem and how you would behave, and how others would behave towards you, and what they would say of you. Talking about life without the difficulty helps you to achieve it as you focus on the future and how life can be for you, helping you think and act more positively.

This type of therapy is useful for a wide range of difficulties including personal, relationship and marital problems, for reaching your full potential, for addictions, depression and for raising your self-esteem.

Narrative therapy

Narrative therapy considers people as the experts in their own lives – they have many skills that will help them solve their difficulties. It also views problems as separate from people – the person is never the problem, the difficulty is the problem; the difficulty is something that you have, not something that defines who you are. And because of this difficulty, you don't have to change who you are but you have to learn how to deal with the effect the difficulty is having on your life.

In recognising that the problem is outside of you, you are 'externalising' it, which will allow you to look upon it with less emotion as you will not see it as criticising your character or as being an inherent part of you that is unchangeable. If working in a family situation, this will help progress as members are less likely to get sidetracked into blame, guilt and defensiveness and will be more able to look upon the problem dispassionately and be critical of the problem rather than of each other. It may also allow room for more inventiveness in finding different ways of seeing things.

Narrative therapy holds the idea that your life and relationships are bound by the stories you tell about them to give meaning to your experiences – and that the way you interpret events to give meaning to them affects you. When you tell stories of your life, you leave out the things that do not tie in with how you see the world because of your particular experiences, prejudices, culture, myths, life rules and beliefs about the world and how you fit into it. So, in telling your story, you are confirming your beliefs about yourself and the world as you skew events to fit your points of view. But there is nothing wrong in doing this – it is something everyone does.

However, there is a problem if how you see yourself and your world causes you pain – such as in thinking that you hate your life and you hate yourself. The therapist will listen to your 'story' to find events that you gloss-over, omit or have forgotten that disprove your unwelcome assumptions, so that together you can rewrite your 'story' into a less painful one. Through having many conversations about your life with the therapist, your reality will change and you can re-author your life and identity to fit with your altered views, making you feel happier about things.

This approach does not ask you to change nor does it try to give you insight as psychodynamic therapy does. It just helps you find a different reality that was always in existence except you weren't able to see it. Narrative therapy can be used as part of family therapy (see page 167).

Motivational interviewing

Motivational interviewing is mainly used to help people who have alcohol, tobacco or drug habits become motivated about changing their ways when they are ambivalent (in two minds about it) or resistant to change. It can also be used to help people who shoplift; who buy items they neither need nor want (for comfort); who need to exercise more or less (if their exercise regime has become obsessive); who need to learn to eat sensibly; who have eating disorders; in marital counselling, and in compliance with medical recommendations.

Motivational interviewing helps you to examine, clarify and resolve feelings about changing your habit or behaviour so that you can successfully make a change, working by eliciting your own self-motivating statements, not the therapist's (this is central to the therapy) in the following key areas.

Self-esteem – you have to have high self-esteem to want to change otherwise you won't see a point to it.

Concern – you need to identify personal concerns over your behaviour and recognise the disadvantages of carrying on without change.

Optimism – you need to have faith in your own abilities, believing you can change.

Knowledge – of the problem (you need to recognise what the problem is), and of strategies (you need to have plans to change).

Desire, intention and commitment to change: you need to want things to be different and know what rewards this will bring – what it'll mean to you and your loved ones; you need to know that you will change and you need to mean to stick with it.

Therapists use your motivational statements to create conflict in you – so that you see how things really are rather than hiding behind unreality. This means that you have to reflect between present behaviour and personal goals. And they notice discrepancies in what you say to increase the conflict so that you voice the need to change yourself. Therapists can use other therapy techniques to help speed up the changes you need to make.

It is up to you to describe how your ambivalence or resistance to change affects you personally so that the therapist can understand your struggles and guide you as an individual towards some kind of resolution to change – through looking at the discrepancies between your current behaviour and your personal goals. This is not the same as persuading you. It is up to you, with help, to find what direction you must take and to find the reasons for taking that direction.

The therapist works collaboratively with you, accepting you as you are, and asks questions to understand your life from your perspective (including your life values and the priorities you attach to each); methods that have been found to diminish resistance to change. There is no place in motivational interviewing for the therapist trying to force you to do something against your will or to create conflict between the two of you, or to pressure you to work at a pace at which you feel uncomfortable.

Family therapy

Family therapy can be of many forms and, within these, therapists do not often stick to the one technique but use techniques from other therapies. The three main schools of family therapy are: strategic family therapy, which involves the therapist negotiating goals with the family and devising tasks for them to carry out; structural family therapy, which involves the therapist looking at the structure of the family and helping them redefine, for example, their role boundaries; and systemic family therapy, which is described below.

In family therapy, the therapist can work with an individual, a couple, the whole family or with part of the family; or have individual meetings as well as meetings with the whole family. The term 'family' is meant loosely – it can include any group of people who live together.

Family therapy provides families with an opportunity to talk about their difficulties in a safe and supported environment. It allows open discussion under guidance by the therapist so that family members can look at their situation with a critical eye and think about things from a new perspective; it can also uncover underlying problems that created the difficulties in the first place. Family therapy relies on finding resources within the family to improve difficulties and to help them get along better.

The consultation can take place in a room with a one-way mirror so that other therapists in the team can watch and support the therapist who is in the room with the family. Sessions may be recorded with the clients' knowledge and permission; these recordings can help the other therapists in the team to discuss the session afterwards.

Systemic family therapy

Systemic family therapy (also known as systemic psycho-therapy, as the techniques can be used for individuals and couples too) is family therapy that draws on something called systemic theory; it has been found to be especially helpful when people have felt stuck in relationship problems.

As well as looking at the systems working within the family – such as couples, children, the family as a unit, the extended family and the effect of previous generations – systemic family therapy looks at wider systems such as social and religious groups, neighbours, friends, and the outside agencies that deal with the family such as social services, doctors, employers and schools: all these systems have an effect on the individual members.

Systemic therapists also need to understand other systems involved in the family such as religion, culture, race, gender, sexual orientation, political beliefs, lifestyle differences, thoughts, attitudes and myths; the therapist may need to ask questions to understand how these affect the family which also helps the family make sense of their world. An awareness of the therapist's, and the therapist's team's, effect on the clients' systems – for example, previous professional and personal experiences – is also required.

Systemic family therapists believe that complex systems, like people, can adapt given encouragement and they operate from a neutral, non-blaming position (looking at the family as a whole, without concentrating on casting blame on an individual). Therapists help to increase the range of choices available to families, and help them to think and act creatively within their particular situation – each family is considered unique. By changing how the family operates, and concentrating on their strengths, families are empowered to solve their own problems.

One of the techniques used in systemic family therapy is circular questioning which involves asking each family member how they think another family member feels about something, revealing differences between them. The knowledge of other family members' viewpoints can stimulate new thinking and helps to bring changes that are beneficial to the whole.

Sessions are constructive rather than destructive: having members see things from other family members' perspectives helps clear up long-term misunderstandings and helps family members see the problem in a different light. As well as allowing family members to clarify their views, circular questioning teaches empathy and learning to accept people as they are despite mistakes that have been made.

The therapist might be able to determine what purpose, if any, the problem serves for the family (it is likely that the person himself has not realised that it does serve a need). For example, if someone is chronically sick and needs looking after, it might serve as a welcome excuse for the carer to sacrifice his own life as he needs to be needed: having such an important role in the family is a way of getting the attention he wants – while bitterly complaining that he has no life.

The therapist may make up a genogram: a diagram showing the family tree with birth and death dates; jobs; significant other dates such as marriage/partnership; divorce/separation; miscarriage/termination dates. This will help in understanding the family structure and significant events that may have affected how it functions.

Looking at the problem from a different perspective is called reframing – in the new light, the situation the client viewed as problematic ceases to be problematic. Positive sides can be recognised. For example, if someone is left alone for many hours because her partner has to work long hours there might come a benefit. It is an opportunity for her to do something that is purely for herself without fear of her partner complaining that she's never around or hasn't fulfilled her commitments to the family. It is valuable time she can make use of rather than thinking it is sterile time that she cannot use because she is incomplete without her partner.

It helps if the problem is externalised so that family members see that they and the problem are separable and that it doesn't need to be always with them. For example, in this book I refer to people as having agoraphobia not that they are agoraphobics; they are not defined by the difficulties they have.

The therapist can also explore what solutions the family

has already tried and whether they were tried in earnest. Other family members may have solutions to suggest that they could later try. Sometimes the therapist may make a suggestion for them to try, although it strengthens the family if they can find their own solutions.

To help motivate the family, the therapist will amplify any observed change to the family so that they see that the definite change is only attributable to the way they have altered their way of doing things; then they can continue doing it that way, and be motivated to look for further solutions to try. This should later lead to family members feeling they have the problem under control and can now deal with that and other problems that might come their way, as they have raised awareness of each other and understand more fully the needs and vulnerabilities of other members, and of themselves.

Neuro-linguistic programming

Neuro-linguistic programming (NLP) is being used in business and education as well as counselling and therapy to help people achieve personal excellence and rapport when dealing with others. There is a core belief in NLP that we all have the resources we need within us.

The founder of systemic psychotherapy, Gregory Bateson, also contributed to the development of NLP and there are some similarities in approaches. For example, both therapies quote 'The map is not the territory': everyone has a map of the world about them but the territory one person sees is very different from what someone else sees because they take their own experiences, culture, interests, language, beliefs, values and expectations into account when they view it.

In arguments between couples, for example, often both sides believe to be in the right while thinking their partners are unfeeling and oblivious of the other's needs. But neither side will realise that they have different territories unless they each explain how they see things and how they feel. Through communication, each can see the other's territory on that particular point, and rapport and understanding will ensue rather than hostility and communication breakdown.

The 'neuro' part of NLP refers to the five senses (sight, hearing, touch, taste and smell) and feelings – subconscious and conscious thoughts and the physiological changes they produce in the body. The 'linguistic' part refers to the internal language people use when talking to themselves and deciding how to behave and the language they use when communicating with others. The 'programming' refers to the way people choose to organise their actions and thoughts to produce results and make sense of the world.

NLP was introduced in *Re-filing your memories* and *Anchors* in Chapter 9 but there are many other therapy techniques used by NLP trained counsellors. One of these is dealing with specific phobias, such as of spiders; the description below has been much simplified.

The therapist will ask you to dissociate yourself from the very first, or earliest, memory you have of your fear of spiders. Then you will be asked to recall a strong and established 'feeling safe and secure' anchor and imagine yourself watching a film clip of your memory when you felt afraid. This dissociates you once from yourself in that memory. Next the therapist will ask you to imagine yourself watching yourself watching the film clip with you in it; this dissociates yourself even further from the memory. The therapist will ask you to pay attention to how your body feels – if you feel the fear rising, you must stop the film clip and fire the anchor for feeling safe and secure.

Then you will be asked to replay the film clip in a darker, quieter mode, in black and white and from a greater distance to reduce the power of the memory. You need to be able to watch the entire clip without experiencing any fear and, when that is achieved, you can associate yourself with yourself again in the present and give yourself time to appreciate how you now feel. To test the change, the therapist will ask you to imagine a time in the future when you might be expected to face your fear again – your fear should now be much reduced.

Part Three

Damaging Influences in Your Life

Life is a series of experiences, each one of which makes us bigger, even though sometimes it is hard to realise this. For the world was built to develop character, and we must learn that the setbacks and grieves which we endure help us in our marching onward.
Henry Ford (1863–1947)

Part Three looks at outside influences that contribute to negative behaviour which is often a measure of how uncomfortable we are with ourselves and with others. Negative behaviour can be either aggressive – such as being threatening, throwing tantrums, undeservedly putting someone down, and being sarcastic or manipulative; or passive – such as being timid or shy, being over-apologetic, agreeing verbally when we mentally disagree, and not being able to say no.

Positive behaviour is assertive behaviour that enables us to interact with other people without causing offence or undue upset; it is dealing with others with respect and consideration, being able to empathise and be non-judgmental. Frequently, people who have had damaging influences in their life have difficulty being assertive and also tend to have low self-esteem.

Once an understanding of how you became the person you are has been achieved, draw a line under your past and concentrate on your future, ensuring that you don't continue along the same negative paths with yourself and with other people. The final chapter helps you accomplish this.

Note
The ideas and suggestions in most of Part Three are from research, personal experience, working in pastoral care and from observing people. The suggestions do not necessarily hold true for everyone emerging from any particular upbringing or familial experience: there are exceptions and other influences impinging on people's lives. However, there is good reason to include these general ideas as, even if you do not feel they apply to you, they may well apply to others around you. Gaining a fuller understanding of human nature and how certain behaviour might come about improves your ability to empathise and be non-judgmental.

16

DAMAGING INFLUENCES IN CHILDHOOD

The family you come from isn't as important as the family you're going to have.
Ring Lardner (1885–1933)

Although your genes have a major part to play in the formation of your personality, the way you choose to express your personality is often determined by the way you were brought up. Any resultant inappropriate behaviour or low self-esteem can prevent you forming lasting and satisfying relationships and adversely affects your ability to be self-reliant.

Once you have understood why your personality has been formed as it has, you are better placed to address your weaknesses and change your approach to life and to the people around you.

Damaging parenting styles
The illustrations below are not intended to criticise or cast blame, but to show why people might behave in certain ways. No one comes from a perfect family. And none of us can ever achieve being a perfect parent – we can only try

our best and hope to learn from some of the mistakes our parents may have made with us. (The word parent relates to whoever happens to be the main carer, providing the most influence on your upbringing.)

Abusive parenting of any kind that clearly amounts to child abuse (where there is significant harm to either a child's physical or mental health) has not been discussed; it is taken as read that it is extremely damaging and can have dire consequences for the child who may have issues including low self-worth, depression, self-harm, promiscuity, aggression, an eating disorder and an inability to trust.

Over-strict parenting

Jacki had very strict parents and was always afraid of doing something wrong in case she was shouted at or hit. She often felt that the punishment she was given far outweighed the transgression. At home, her behaviour became exemplary: she was extremely diligent and acquiescent, far too scared of the consequences to do wrong. She lived in fear of never sufficiently pleasing her parents or coming up to their over-high expectations, too timid to make her needs known or to ask for anything important.

Naturally gentle, Jacki was made shy and withdrawn by her upbringing, finding it hard to look people in the eye. Her behaviour identified her as a 'victim', unconsciously inviting people to take advantage of her and bully her. It was also difficult for her to talk to others as an equal, even when she became adult, particularly to those in authority as she lacked self-confidence and self-esteem.

Being brought up in a closely controlled way gave Jacki little opportunity to explore her world. Since her freedom was severely restricted, her experiences were limited which meant that she remained dependent and nervous as an adult unlike her friends who were happy to become independent and live away from home. When problems arose in Jacki's life she quickly buckled under the stress, never having built the confidence to tackle them or learnt how to survive them.

Hadyn had a similar upbringing to Jacki but had a more resilient nature. He became aggressive and fought against the unfair parenting he had, by refusing to listen, slamming doors and walking out of the house. He bullied children at school that he considered more vulnerable than himself, and later colleagues at work. After his marriage, he also started to bully his wife and treat their children unfairly. Although Hadyn considered himself confident he had low self-esteem – he felt his parents were never happy with him, making him feel a failure.

Ellie also had very strict parents but she became very secretive and led a life outside the home of which her parents knew nothing. In response to her experiences at home, she grew to be underhand, sly and manipulative. Once completely away from the restrictive ruling of her parents, Ellie became wild and did many things she had never been allowed to do before; at university she binged on alcohol and became promiscuous. The sudden freedom got out of hand and Ellie was unable to practise sufficient self-discipline to complete the course successfully.

Over-lax parenting

Fraser was rarely disciplined so lacked the ability to keep his negative behaviour in check to conform to what society expected of him. Lacking in self-discipline, Fraser found it hard to stick with a task until it was finished which affected his exam results. Despite getting low grades, his parents did not chastise him; they merely showed disappointment. Sometimes Fraser suspected his parents didn't sufficiently care about him to be bothered with putting him right and this made him feel unworthy of their attention, giving him low self-esteem.

Fraser resorted to aggressive and anti-social behaviour as part of a gang, happy that he could strongly identify with the group. Through what they did together, he got the respect, recognition and sense of belonging he craved.

Spoiling parents

Jan's parents did everything for her and gave her what she wanted whenever it was within their means to do so, without her having to wait or save for it. They also gave her whatever attention she wanted whenever they could. This made her cavalier in her attitude towards her parents' availability long into adulthood and she was careless of her finances, never having experienced the need to budget carefully. Never having learnt to take responsibility for her own mistakes, Jan always expected her parents to bail her out of trouble.

When things didn't go right for Jan or if she couldn't get her own way, she became aggressive. She found it hard to see other people's points of view or to empathise with them, and rarely considered other people's feelings, whining and cajoling until she got what she wanted. She was not good at listening – frequently interrupting conversations – was impatient, easily bored, and was only interested in herself.

However, Jan did have a great deal of self-confidence and had high self-esteem since her parents had always shown how much she meant to them. But she had difficulty understanding why others did not revere her in the same way, expecting continued respect from whomever she met, without earning it. Motivation was also a problem for her as her parents rarely scolded her. If they did suggest that Jan had not done her best, she would throw a tantrum – so trying to get her to achieve her potential was not worth the trouble.

Melissa's parents were away on business a great deal and she had a stream of different carers: as soon as she got used to and attached to one, that nanny left and was replaced by another, making her feel insecure. Fearing she would get hurt if she allowed herself to care, Melissa became wary of forming close relationships. Her self-esteem was low: she felt she was not good enough or interesting enough for her parents to want to spend time with her and to be interested in what she did. Occasionally she was angry and aggressive, deliberately doing things to shock her parents just to get noticed.

As Melissa always got what she wanted materially, she expected the rest of things that she wanted in life to come easily such as passing exams and gaining qualifications. But she was poorly motivated as she was guaranteed a job in her parents' company and was not a high achiever.

Denied the personal success that comes with having worked for something of her very own, Melissa was very passive – life was all too easy, with everything either being done for her or handed to her without her having to make a huge effort in rising to challenges. Anything that required great effort, Melissa passed by.

Uninterested parents

Rob was largely ignored by his parents and he considered this to be worse than being disliked or smothered with affection. It made Rob behave in an anti-social way, to get himself noticed, feeling that getting into trouble and having his parents' anger focused on him was preferable to not having any attention at all.

But Marie, who had experienced the same type of

parenting as Rob, was made passive, responding to people by not expecting to be noticed, not expecting to succeed and not expecting to have her company sought or enjoyed. Her self-esteem was extremely low. What made it worse was that her parents didn't mete out the same treatment to her older brother; they talked to him more and showed him more interest and concern.

Closely controlling parents

Piers' father ran their home like a regiment. If Piers stepped out of line by failing to look smart, be punctual, get good grades or be polite, his father would become enraged. Piers had to show he could take the punishment dished out – showing he had a 'stiff upper lip' or could take it 'like a man' – and if he didn't, he was sneered at for being a snivelling weakling.

Piers was not allowed to develop at his own pace, in his own way or to profit from making mistakes through self-discovery. He also wasn't allowed to show feelings of vulnerability or give vent to his anger, which made him aggressive in adulthood, meting out the same treatment to his own offspring. His experience could also have crushed him making him passive, but in either case, he would have low self-esteem because his needs had not been acknowledged or recognised; they were always secondary to his father's needs.

Matt had very vigilant parents who were always watching him for signs of sinning, telling him what would happen should he break certain commandments or rules. This made him feel that his parents did not trust him, lowering his self-esteem.

Blindly following the Christian religious doctrines that his parents thrust at him made Matt passive with low self-esteem. 'Turn the other cheek' gave him the message that he was not worth protecting and that he must allow others to take advantage of him. 'The meek shall inherit the earth' encouraged him to wait until death for higher goals rather than strive now to achieve his full potential.

Effects of family background

If you were a member of a family that never had enough money for school trips, decent clothes, and celebratory events, you may have felt shamed and embarrassed. You may also have felt embarrassed about asking anyone to visit your home. The state of your furnishings, or the district in which you lived, may have been so deprived that you did not want anyone else to see it. You may have had to make excuses as to why you couldn't go out to the cinema with your friends, not wanting to admit you hadn't any money.

You may still be making excuses about money, ashamed to admit you are struggling to survive and to feed your own children. Or you might have tried to hide any feelings of being uncomfortable and different from your friends by pretending you were simply not interested in good clothes or in going out with them. These things are liable to give you low self-esteem and low self-confidence.

If people who had more money than you treated you as though you were of no consequence, you could have become aggressive to try to hide your jealousy of other people's lifestyles – or because no one had ever cared well for you and you knew that you had only yourself and your wits to rely on in the world.

Perhaps your family was wealthy and you had a house-keeper and servants. If you needed anything, you only had to ask. Knowing you had 'status' may have made you very self-confident. You could probably easily stand up for yourself and make your needs known, having high self-esteem but it could easily overspill into arrogance, finding it hard to accept that others have an equal right to the respect and consideration you feel yourself worthy of.

You may have had more freedom to take risks, knowing that there would always be someone to bail you out of trouble, knowing that you were going to be OK and not caring what happened to anyone else whom you might affect. You may believe that money can buy everything: if you throw enough money at someone you can persuade him to do whatever you want. But if suddenly, for some reason, you are without money you might find it hard adjusting to being in a subordinate role as an employee of a company not owned by a family member.

Similar to the financial status examples, the position in society that your family holds can affect your self-esteem and behaviour. For example, if your parents are high-ranking officials, or royalty with certain privileges, you might experience similar consequences as the wealthy. But if your parents' jobs have low status or they have no jobs, or there is something else that sets your family apart from others in the area, society is often cruel and judgmental, shaming or shunning them. This can rub off on to you and the consequences may be similar to those experienced as the poor.

Effects of gender

You are brought up according to your gender role – the expectations people have of you because of being born either a girl or a boy. These include aspects of behaviour, appearance, subject choices, career choices, lifestyle, choice of sexual partner and your personality.

Boys are encouraged to be lively, outgoing, adventurous, tough, fit and strong. The expectation is that they are louder, noisier, messier and more aggressive than girls and that they should like, and be good at, sport. To be a 'man' it is largely thought you must stand up for yourself, fight for your rights (verbally and physically) and not show any weaknesses or vulnerable emotions such as fear and upset, or speak about your feelings.

There is great pressure on men not to be 'gay' – anyone who is may be made to feel weak and ashamed, the target of abuse and violence. Macho men seem to have little tolerance for homosexuals, bisexuals, transsexuals and those who are intersex – people whose sexuality is ambiguous (see Chapter 18). The more sensitive nature of a man is rarely seen as a positive attribute. Yet sensitivity is seen as a positive attribute in women – and women are considered unfeminine if they aren't sensitive. Men are expected to be the main earners in a family and not have the major part in childcare: it is more unusual for a father to take a career break to look after babies while the mother goes out to work.

Some men may be aggressive to live up to 'macho' expectations. This may affect their relationships by not getting beyond superficiality – their friendships tend to be less intimate and they tend to disclose less about their personal lives and how they feel than most women do. This may prevent them from reaching a deep understanding of others. Other men may feel cowed by the fact that they cannot behave in a macho way. Feeling that they should be macho, but aren't, may make them timid, ashamed that they, too, can't be a 'man'. The pressure to behave like a 'man' may make them very unhappy with themselves, giving them low self-esteem.

Girls are encouraged to be caring and careful, neat and tidy, to be polite and listen, and to behave like a 'lady'. The less feminine a woman is considered to be, the more she

can expect to be abused for it. Lesbians, bisexuals, transsexuals and those who are intersex, like gay men, are not
well tolerated by society and are the target of many
unkind words and acts.

In a male-dominated career, women may have to fight
harder and be *much* better than men going for the same
job to secure it for themselves. High-flying career women
tend to be more aggressive than men – and have to be to
get and stay where they want to be in today's society.

Passive women may limit their horizons and not consider life choices that are thought of as traditionally to be
a man's domain. Women who stick to their traditional
roles may be so rewarded through praise because of doing
what is expected of them – fulfilling the stereotypical role
– that they lose motivation to seek out more for themselves
even though they may want more. Women who depart
from what is expected of them are often made to feel bad
about themselves, which lowers their self-esteem.

Effects of parental separation and divorce

Boys and girls whose parents have divorced are more likely
to suffer from behavioural problems such as disruptive
behaviour, precocious sexual activity, destruction of property, refusal to do homework, breaking school rules and
dropping out of school. They are also more likely to suffer
emotional problems such as anger, a lack of trust, refusal
to accept responsibility for their actions and decisions, and
low self-esteem.

In young adulthood, the children of divorced parents
are more likely to have social problems, having trouble
forming and maintaining close relationships. Girls are
more likely to have internalised problems that include
withdrawal, depression and anxiety (which lead to passivity) whereas boys are more likely to have externalised

problems such as anti-social activities, verbal and physical aggression, rejection of authority and non-compliance (all of which are aggressive).

Effects of being very dependent

Perhaps you had, or still have, a serious illness or severe disability and were very dependent on your parents for your treatment, your frequent visits to the doctor and the hospital, and could not have survived without their help. You knew that looking after you took up a great chunk of their lives and you felt guilty about it.

This could have made you passive as it was hard for you to ask more of your parents or make different needs known to them, putting your emotional needs far lower down the list than you would have done had you been healthy and more independent. (This also applies to being cared for later in life by a partner, or a child.) Or it could have made you angry that you couldn't be like everyone else, feeling bitter with your lot in life. Or you could swing between being passive in your weaker, more vulnerable moments and aggressive when frustration and anger hit. Being different from the majority can lower your self-esteem, particularly if you are dependent on others. However, it is possible to focus on other qualities and improve them to raise your self-esteem.

The ideal family

If you were very lucky, both your parents were assertive and you copied their positive behaviour by observing what they did, what they said and how they did and said these things. You knew that when your mother or father shouted at you there was good reason. They would always explain why they were angry and then listen to your side of the matter. You thought your parents were fair with their punishment and in what they said.

You were discouraged from underhand behaviour: if you wanted something, you had to be direct. This didn't mean you always got your own way but it did mean your parents took the time to listen to you and recognised your needs. There was mutual respect.

When your parents argued, they always stuck to the point without saying unkind things that had nothing to do with whatever started the argument. They tried to understand each other's needs better: they never walked out when the other was in mid-sentence because they could not face what was being said and they never threw tantrums for the sake of it. If they got angry, it was always over something important.

This type of upbringing gives you self-respect and respect for others because that's how you were treated, and you would have an excellent self-esteem. But, in reality, it is very unlikely that people can stick to the behaviour described.

Ideally, we should all be self-confident, happy, out-going people who are ready to meet new challenges, with no need to strike out when things go wrong or hide away in fear and despair. But few of us are truly this self-confident and at ease with ourselves. We rely on the security from home and our parents well into adulthood. If we are lucky, we are happy to leave home when the time comes and get our comfort and security from our friends and, later, a partner. Later still, if things go wrong, and if we are lucky, we learn to rely on ourselves – such as after a divorce or death of our partner. This process can take years to transpire and the idea of relying on oneself can be very daunting, so you need all the help you can get in forming true, meaningful relationships.

17

DAMAGING INFLUENCES IN ADULTHOOD

*Difficulties are meant to rouse, not discourage. The human
spirit is to grow strong by conflict.*
William Ellery Channing (1780–1842)

This chapter concentrates on examples of outside influences that affect your self-esteem and behaviour in your working life – whether or not you are in paid work – and later, in old age.

Since some aspects of your adulthood may be similar to those described in Chapter 16, they have not been repeated here. For example, you may remain in the same financial situation or have the same social status as when you were a child, or you may become romantically involved with someone who takes over one of the parental roles previously described.

Men and women at work
In many jobs, just a modicum of knowing how to handle people and their complaints is needed. However, there are many jobs where this balanced middle ground is *not* required, where it is actually necessary for the success in

your chosen career to be either aggressive or passive. If you are happy in these roles, your self-esteem will not suffer, but if they are contrary to your nature, your self-esteem will diminish.

Careers that demand aggression would not suit a person who is timid and shy. Journalism, for example, is a very popular career and the competition is high, but you do need to be pushy to make a success of it. Union leaders need to be able to support their members and need to be forceful to bring about changes; they need to make their voices heard. Sales representatives often need to sell to get paid through commission; if they don't successfully press for a sale, they aren't paid – or just a very low base wage.

Senior managers need to be able to deal effectively with issues brought up by other staff members, push for deadlines to be kept and be able to hold on to their senior positions by constantly proving their worth and their ability to do the job. Politicians need to voice their policies and opinions with energy and conviction and regularly have to speak in front of an audience; they always have to show outward strength.

If you work in a place where competition is high and there is much hiring and firing resulting in a large staff turnover, you may feel you have to be first and best at everything to keep your position. If you want very quick promotion, you have to work at pushing yourself forward all the time to be noticed, to stand apart from everyone else and have a single aim in mind: that of getting what you want. However, it is possible to work hard and be noticed without being aggressive.

Careers that demand passivity would not suit an aggressive or assertive person; employers expect or demand you to be in a subordinate role without fighting against the system. For example, in the armed forces, you are trained to obey commands without hesitation. Making your own decisions about whether something is right or wrong is actively discouraged. Here, you are being forced to be submissive.

In office work, your employers want you to do as you're asked; you won't get very far if you question your boss all the time or refuse to do something. Apprentices learn a skill or trade under supervision and are expected to take instruction from those more experienced. Nuns, priests and monks are also expected to be submissive, accepting guidance from their superiors.

Generally, if you work for an employer in the employer's environment you are expected to be passive – bearing in mind the exceptions mentioned above where the careers do demand some aggression. There are also many careers or situations where there is strict hierarchy that you need to observe to do well. For example, you may be able to call your immediate boss by her first name, but none above her. Or you may only be allowed to take your ideas up to a certain level as above this is reserved for people higher up the scale. There are hierarchies in most societal structures – in many religions, in uniformed work, in big companies and in the monarchy.

How your colleagues treat you

If you are bullied, treated without respect or are always being passed over when it comes to promotion, you are likely to be passive. However, if you are treated with respect, your opinions sought and you are regularly consulted over departmental issues you are likely to have high self-esteem, be more self-confident and so be more willing to risk standing up for yourself and making your needs known.

How people judge you

People often judge your worth by the job you hold. If you are in a responsible job that has demanded numerous qualifications, you may anticipate more respect from those around you. This may make you self-confident and able to stick up for yourself. But it might also make you arrogant, believing you are better than other people, deserving immediate attention, the best available service and extra consideration because of your position.

If you are in an unskilled job you may not be able to command the same sort of presence as one who is in a highly responsible job. You may try to compensate by being arrogant, making sure everyone knows that you won't be taken advantage of. You may have what is described as a 'chip on your shoulder'. Or you may feel inferior to those around you and think things like, 'I couldn't possibly disturb her, she's much too busy – and her job is so much more important than mine.'

If you are unemployed, you may experience shame at not having a job as though it were a public declaration of unworthiness or unsuitability. This could make you very defensive about your position or it might make you become depressed and disheartened about being unemployed. Often people do not see beyond the superficiality of the job to the person inside and see what merit lies there. It is an extra effort to have to prove your worth to others when they do not regard you sympathetically.

If you are promoted above your ability, you may struggle to keep ahead with your work. The constant pressure not to be found struggling with your work, or to provide the work on time, may dash your self-confidence so that you dread meetings and dealing with your colleagues. Being constantly reminded that the people you work with are so much more able than you is likely to make you timid and apologetic and lower your self-esteem. However, you may feel you need to protect your 'patch', to keep others at bay so that you remain undiscovered or even try to counter their criticism by looking for flaws in their work. This is likely to result in a workplace war, with much backbiting and everyone waiting for you to make the next blunder, which would further lower your self-esteem.

Effects of other significant people

The closer people are to you, the greater their influence. (Damaging parenting styles were looked at in Chapter 16.)

Partners who do not take you seriously, put you down at every opportunity, abuse you or threaten you, are more likely to make you timid, lacking in self-confidence and self-esteem. If you are expected to do more than your fair share of the housework, while your partner makes all decisions for you and does not consult you over things that affect your life, your home or the children (if you have them), your low self-esteem would make it hard for you to be assertive, to insist on things being more equal between you.

If your partner is very timid and does not check your negative behaviour, you may take advantage of his gentle and non-confrontational temperament. But you may not feel proud of yourself for behaving like this, damaging your own self-esteem.

Parents-in-law – of any stable relationship – can have very high expectations of their offspring's partner which they may make clear to you that you don't fulfil. You might be resentful, knowing that you have fallen short of their ideal, and become aggressive towards them. Or they might effectively ignore you whenever possible, showing interest only in your partner, failing to acknowledge your birthday or important things that have happened in your life. The extent of damage to your self-esteem depends on your frequency of contact with them.

In-laws may also disapprove of your lifestyle and how you bring up your children – if you have any and, if you don't, they may disapprove of your being childless. This may cause problems between you and your partner, which may make you feel even more angry and resentful towards your in-laws, fostering aggression and feelings of unworthiness.

If your in-laws are over-helpful, bending over backwards to give you assistance in every conceivable way you might be annoyed with them, wanting to live your own life and make your own decisions. Or you may be grateful to have all your worries taken care of with little or no effort on your part. But this could lower your self-esteem, as you cannot be proud of coping largely by yourself.

Brothers and sisters-in law can also make your life hard; they may be jealous of you, wishing, for example, they could have your lifestyle, which can lead to discord and resentment, with you feeling the need to be wary of traps and deliberate troublemaking.

Children can contribute to healthy parental self-esteem by doing things you are proud of such as being kind and loving. Giving your children high self-esteem, such as by frequently praising them regardless of how they compare to other children their age, helps give you high self-esteem too. If you need to compare, compare with how they were a year ago and praise any step forward.

Having a child with a disability or special needs could create tension in the home because of the extra burden put upon you. This may make you buckle under the strain, feeling unable to cope, or it may make you angry that life should be so hard for you all: people's reaction to your child or her behaviour may make you angry towards them.

Or you may cope very well, strengthening your belief in yourself and giving you high self-esteem and self-confidence.

If your child is being bullied or treated unfairly for any reason, you are likely to get mad to protect her. Should you experience the death or severe illness of a child, the experience may crush you or make you bitter and jealous of others with live, healthy children.

Elderly parents can be burdensome to look after and you may feel you are unable to cope, life having worn you down or it may make you resentful, snapping at everyone else because your needs have been put aside for too long.

Friends who are supportive and obviously enjoy your company are likely to make you self-confident with high self-esteem. However, if you are very popular and you have never had to work hard at your friendships, you may take them for granted and be arrogant and over-confident – albeit with high self-esteem. This type of behaviour may be used to control others such as in being the leader of some sort of gang where you coerce others weaker than yourself to do things against their will in order to stay in the friendship group.

If your friends patronise you, never praise you, don't seek your opinion, don't ask you for advice or keep your confidences, you are likely to be timid, lack self-confidence and have low self-esteem. Or you may not have any friends at all which may also dash your self-confidence and self-esteem, making you passive. However, it is possible that, because you are unused to having people be friendly towards you, you react suspiciously to any overtures of friendship with aggression, driving people further away.

If you have had many negative social experiences, you may have developed social phobia, protecting yourself from further hurt and criticism by withdrawing from other people, not daring to take the risks involved with making friends for fear it will go wrong in some way and cause you further emotional pain.

Effects of poor health

Feeling unwell much of the time drains you and reduces your self-confidence as you might wonder how you are to get through each day. Any additional problem that arises might fill you with panic, knowing you cannot cope with anything else. This is likely to make you passive and lower your self-esteem.

If you have poor mental health such as suffering from an anxiety disorder, each day may fill you with such dread that you have lost all self-confidence and self-esteem. You may also have the added burden of trying to hide your psychological distress from others, fearing their contempt and ridicule of you.

If you are always tired or in pain, you are likely to have a short fuse, quickly snapping back at people. Although you may be aware that your behaviour is unacceptable, you may feel unable to change, disliking yourself for it, further lowering your self-esteem.

Adapting to any great downward change in your health is hard. To become suddenly blind, have a disability or have a terminal illness involves much adaptation of your life, having to come to terms with what has happened to you – and any related prejudice and discrimination you might come across. You might wonder how you are going to cope, your self-confidence plummeting, or the experience may have embittered you. Or you might swing between the two. Unless you can find something you can still do well and excel in, your self-esteem may remain low. It is usually very important to people to feel able to contribute to their environment and their loved ones: to help provide income and assist in daily chores.

Middle to old age

As you get older, you probably gain self-confidence because you have had more experience of dealing with people and have seen more of life and lived through more stressful situations such as the ones described above.

Other things, such as experiencing an emotional breakdown, may reduce your self-confidence and self-esteem despite having lived through it and having your life back to 'normal'. The memory of that time may live on and haunt you, threatening your equilibrium if you feel pressures building up again. However, you will probably understand yourself much better and be more forgiving of your weaknesses, so you will still have moved on and progressed to another level in your life's journey.

Some examples of life stresses that an older person may well have personally experienced or known of someone close to them experiencing are: addictions, bankruptcy, burglary, being conned, being mugged, being unhappily childless, bereavement, causing serious injury or death to someone else, committing a crime (and getting caught), divorce, eviction, experiencing war, being involved in a crash, a house fire or flood, serving a jail sentence, loneliness, miscarriage and termination, one or more major operations, rape, redundancy, repossession of the family home, sexual problems and suicide of someone close. These examples could, of course, be experienced by younger people but perhaps not in the same quantities as in an older person.

On a more uplifting note, an older person may have had

many positive experiences, which add to their self-confidence and aid their ability to deal with problems. Some examples are: being promoted to a high level, being socially experienced, being used to dealing with people, finding pleasure in being alone, finding strength in religion, having brought up many children, having experience of going places alone, having grandchildren, having hobbies to occupy them after retirement, having learned other languages, having looked after health and body, having saved for old age, having a supportive friendship group and having widely travelled.

All positive things increase your self-confidence and self-esteem, and your ability to be assertive and look after your best interests. The negative things have also served to increase your self-confidence, as long as you survived them and didn't become emotionally crushed by them.

However, if you have experienced a very tough life, you may verge on the aggressive and not deal as sensitively with people as you might otherwise. You may not 'suffer fools gladly' or have patience with anyone who appears to be weaker than you in some way. You may feel that because you survived, others should be able to do likewise. Having high self-esteem and being very self-confident may make you less tolerant of others and damage their self-esteem.

If you are dependent on carers – family members or professional carers – who make you feel apologetic for your existence you may be unable to make many of your needs known, believing that you are too insignificant to bother anyone else.

A possible way forward from here is to consider what you can or *do* do for family caring for you and what you have a right to expect in exchange. Remind yourself of all the things you have done for them over the years and ask if their treatment of you is fair. The more apologetic you are, the more your carers will feel that they have a right to complain and the lower your self-esteem becomes – it also increases the risk of elderly abuse.

18

DAMAGING INFLUENCES OF RELIGION AND CULTURE

I am not an Athenian or a Greek but a citizen of the world.
Socrates (469–399 BC)

It is sometimes your experience of religion and culture that can negatively affect your behaviour and self-esteem. Although many people embrace the values and traditions that are part of their familial experience, others fall foul of them believing that they have been poorly treated compared with others on the planet, particularly in the case of women and girls being treated differently from men and boys.

Men and women in a multi-faith world
It is generally understood that many religions have not given women equal status to men because when these religions were first developed, women did not have a high status in society. Also, the translations of religious texts were always undertaken by men, who interpreted them in the light of their own male-oriented beliefs. Although society has now changed, many religions are resisting change because certain traditions are thought of as having

been laid down by God and because the men who hold the power within their religion do not want to relinquish control.

In this section, certain aspects within the major world religions have been looked at to show how women are regarded; some of the information was drawn from *Women in Religion*, edited by Jean Holm with John Bowker, published by Continuum 1994 in London and New York. These isolated pieces of information are out of context of the religion in its entirety and are not in any way meant to define the religion as either positive or negative.

In the religions and/or cultures where women are of unequal status, their self-esteem is more likely to be low and passivity may be encouraged or even demanded.

In Buddhism, nuns have never been given the same status as monks, the most senior nun being subordinate to the most recently ordained monk; and they are not allowed to teach monks, regardless of how highly educated they are. They are often poor as their lower status doesn't attract donations: consequently the education of future nuns has been threatened throughout the centuries. Another indication of how women are regarded in Buddhism is given by the fact that, in Thailand for example, there are special places on buses reserved for monks so that they are not obliged to sit next to a woman.

Lay Buddhism is much easier for women to become involved in than monastic Buddhism: meditation centres can provide childcare facilities to allow them the opportunity to take a break in their domestic life for meditation and study; and some well-educated lay women have begun to teach and lead their communities.

In Christianity – as in Judaism – the burden of the first sin was given to a woman, Eve. Some men, who take the

Old Testament of the Bible literally, may attribute lack of self-control on their part to a woman being a 'temptress'.

Some religious teachings that advise against women preachers, or against allowing women to have a say, are found in the New Testament. In 1 Timothy 2.11 it is written: 'Let a woman learn in silence with all submissiveness' and in 1 Timothy 2:12, it is written: 'I permit no woman to teach or have authority over men; she is to keep silent.' Perpetuating these 'teachings', or taking them literally, despite the social changes wrought since they were written, allows men to continue having greater religious authority over women, making women feel they are less worthy than men.

Women priests are not allowed in the Roman Catholic Church but they are permitted, for example, in the Anglican, Methodist and Baptist Churches. Women have always been treated as men's equals in the Quaker Church.

In strongly Roman Catholic countries, women's lives are made hard by religious and political laws limiting access to contraception and abortion. Some women in these countries give birth to children knowing they cannot adequately feed or clothe them and are often made ill from bearing so many children.

In Hinduism, many religious texts put women down and suggest they are inferior to men such as the *Devi Bhagavata 1.5.83*: 'A woman is the embodiment of rashness and a mine of vices . . . she is an obstacle to the path of devotion, a hindrance to emancipation . . . she is practically a sorceress and represents vile desire.' The idea of women being temptresses is similar to the Christian religion. As a mother, a woman is revered, but as a sexual partner she is seen as an obstacle to man's spiritual quest.

In the Dharmasastras, the legal texts, women are classified with the lowest class, irrespective of their social class or origin and are considered ritually impure – because of menstruation – and therefore not entitled to study religion or recite the sacred mantras.

It is a wife's duty to be devoted to her husband and obey him; and she does not have a separate existence apart from him. In the past, this led to *sati*, where a widow burned on the funeral pyre with her husband to become virtuous, but it is very rare today. Widows were considered bad luck and were not welcome at festivals, social and religious ceremonies, although this is not always the case today.

Daily worship, religious festivals and fasts are centred on the home – rather than the temple which is virtually the domain of male priests only – and women have a pivotal role in performing rituals on behalf of the family and in the religious education of their children.

Hindus have a class system of four castes, of which there can be subgroups, where there are detailed rules for its members – of both sexes – regarding food, marriage and occupation. But there is another group Hindus are believed to be born into outside of these castes known as the 'outsiders'; these people are considered too lowly to be in the caste system. 'Outsiders' are also known as the 'untouchables' or dalits – Hindus believe that touching them is polluting – and they make up about a fifth of the Indian population. Untouchables, believed to be born outsiders because of an accumulation of sins in past lives, can only have the most menial jobs and are open to being attacked, abused, murdered and raped; young girls may be forced into prostitution.

Although 'untouchability' was abolished over fifty years ago, Hindus still continue to discriminate against the untouchables.

In Islam (Islam being the Arabic word for 'submit', referring to submission to the will of God), some of the ruling comes not from the Qur'an itself but from interpretation men have given it and from Islamic culture. For example, the Qur'an says that women should 'guard their private parts' and 'cast their veils over their bosoms' or 'draw their veils close to them'. It does not say that women should be covered completely or that they should cover their heads. Women's veils used to be ornamental scarves: it is supposed that originally women who were rich enough to be idle covered their heads as a sign that they did not have to work.

When women attend Friday worship, they are segregated from the men and must pray in a section behind the men or in a gallery to the rear of the main hall. Women can only lead the prayers for other women and only in the absence of a man but it has been documented that the Prophet Muhammad appointed a woman to lead the prayers for both the men and the women of his household.

The relationship between Muslim society and Muslim law is complex. Some social practices may be assumed by the followers of Islam to be part of Muslim law when they are not. For example, many Muslim women are denied education, their legal inheritance and their entitlement to economic independence because they are ignorant of the law and assume that conservative local tradition is identical with Muslim law when in reality such traditions are the inversions of the law.

Despite the Qur'an stating that morally and spiritually men and women, husbands and wives are equal, Muslim legislators have brought their own interpretations into making laws such as saying that a woman may not leave her husband without her husband's permission: in some Muslim countries today even a wife of, say, a government minister, may not leave the country without her husband's written permission. The Qur'an's ruling on adultery (*Surah*

24:3 Asad) holds both partners equally to blame – as with their interpretation of the story of Adam and Eve – and does not decree the stoning to death of women as Sunni law advocates (following the Biblical law of Moses).

The Qur'an states that men have authority over women because they are superior and because they spend their wealth to maintain them – and that husbands are allowed to beat their wives into submission. It also states that good women are obedient, encouraging passivity and discouraging women to make a stand and to try to change things for the better (from the Qur'an, *Surah* 4:34).

The Muslim belief in predestination – that God controls everything – may mean that both men and women may accept what is happening to them without trying to change it: that is, to act passively. This may make a person feel powerless and ineffectual: he or she may react to a tragic event by saying, 'It is God's will' ('Insh'Allah').

Islam assumes that children will follow the religious faith of their father. While a Muslim man can take a Jewish or Christian bride, Muslim women cannot marry outside the faith.

It is written in the Qur'an that a man can take up to four wives: as long as he treats them equally. This was intended to provide protection and a home for widows rather than giving men licence to have more than one wife. Indeed, it later states that it is preferable for men only to have one wife. If the husband agrees, a Muslim woman can secure a marriage contract that ensures she remains the only wife.

In Judaism, one of the blessings made by an Orthodox male Jew is thanking God for not having made him a woman: 'Blessed are you Lord our God, King of the Universe, who has not made me a woman', suggesting that women are considered second rate in Judaism.

A married couple is not allowed to have intercourse

while the woman is menstruating, as women are considered unclean during this time. Orthodox women must wait seven days after their menstrual flow has ceased before cleansing: then sexual relations can resume. Women are also considered unclean for a time after a child is born: the period varying depending on whether the baby is a boy or a girl. The period of being unclean for a girl birth is longer than that for a boy birth. These rules may make a woman feel disgusted and revolted by her natural bodily functions, reducing her self-esteem.

As in Islam, Jewish women are seated away from the men during communal worship. The main prayer area of an orthodox synagogue is divided into male and female sections, separated by a partition. The women's section is frequently on a balcony or at the back of the room, the partition often impeding the view of the service that always takes place in the men's section. The Torah scrolls and other holy objects are kept in the men's section.

In Orthodox Judaism, women are allowed to conduct services and read from the Torah but only for themselves and for each other, not for a mixed congregation. Women can only become non-orthodox rabbis. Women are exempt from the twice-daily praying in the synagogue expected of devout Jewish men, as they are expected to spend more time in the home: their worship is intended to be more private and personal.

Sikhism is one of the world's youngest religions and is the first religion to give equal status to women in social, religious, political and administrative areas. A Sikh woman is an individual in her own right: she does not have to take her husband's name and is fully involved in worship, being permitted to take part in leading and reading prayers and reciting the scriptures to a congregation of both sexes.

But although religious teachings say that men and women should equally share influential positions and domestic work, in reality this is not always the case. There are few Sikh women who are secretaries or presidents of management committees of their gurdwaras – places of worship – and although both men and women share cooking, cleaning and the serving of food to Sikh Gurus in the gurdwaras, many men do not share domestic chores at home even when both partners work.

Sikh women are not to wear a veil to cover their faces or live in seclusion and female infanticide is forbidden, as is association with anyone who practises it. Every Sikh is commanded to lead a married life and all but one Sikh Guru set up homes and led married lives with their families. There are no priests, hierarchy or ordained ministry: Sikhs believe that anyone has direct access to God and worship is part of everyday life in a family setting – unlike other religions where people might leave the community to devote their life to God.

Men and women in a multi-cultural world

Many women find it hard or impossible to be assertive, usually because of a lack of self-confidence and low self-esteem. It may be because of their personality – but men, too can have such vulnerabilities – or because of the way they are regarded in society and the way in which people relate to them. More women tend to be passive than aggressive if they are not assertive. This section suggests some reasons why.

There are a great many inequalities all over the world in the treatment of women. Throughout history women have been largely undervalued and have had poor status. This affects the way they see themselves and the way others treat them. For example, all over the world many more women (and girls) are raped than men (and boys) and many women suffer domestic violence at the hands of men, which demonstrates the object value some men hold for women.

Domestic violence against women is widespread in Pakistan and includes physical abuse, rape and gang rape, acid throwing, burning and killing – in what is termed 'honour killings' by male relatives when they suspect the woman of having an affair, if she files for divorce, is a victim of rape or gets married without their consent. Some women in Kashmir have had acid sprayed onto their faces for not wearing the veil and for not following strict Islamic dress code.

A Hindu wife's status is very much increased if she gives birth to a boy and is raised to a lesser extent on the birth of a girl, probably because of religious reasons – being impure, and economic reasons – having to provide a dowry.

Despite the custom of dowry being forbidden by law, it still continues and the status of a woman in her husband's family can depend on the value of her dowry. Thousands of Hindu women are burnt to death each year in India because their dowries are insufficient. The victims' families put these burnings down to the woman catching fire in her kitchen while she is cooking. In Pakistan, Muslim and Christian women are being burned in what is termed 'stove burnings' – kerosene oil has been thrown at them before they are set fire to: sometimes, the woman is burnt by her brother because she has fallen in love or by her husband because he wants a new wife.

Many men in many cultures who have been promiscuous have double standards, demanding that the woman they make their wife must be a virgin. A woman, in their eyes, is instantly devalued if she is unmarried and has had sex with a man.

Some girls, especially in South Asia and West Africa, are married against their will as young as ten into a life of effective slavery. Many of them are abused and some die at their husband's hands.

Female genital mutilation has been widely reported to be taking place in many African countries and parts of the Middle East. This may be female circumcision (the removal of the woman's clitoris) or infibulation (the removal of the clitoris, labia minora and all or part of the labia majora): the vagina is then stitched up, allowing a small hole to remain for the menstrual blood to escape. In many African societies, a woman cannot get married unless she is infibulated. The hole from the infibulation must be cut open and resealed when the husband wants sex (he may have more than one wife) and when the woman gives birth.

The practice of selective termination of pregnancies to expel female foetuses and the murder of baby girls soon after birth, and the deliberate neglect of very young girls – leading to death – has been widely documented. Genetic testing for sex selection, although made illegal in India in 1996, is still widely reported to continue.

According to UNESCO, two thirds of the 862 million illiterate adults in the world in 2000 were women. Millions of girls have no education at all, especially in countries such as Burkina Faso, Burundi, Mali, Niger, Nepal, Pakistan and Yemen.

Often in developing countries women have low status, not being permitted to own land, inherit property or qualify for credit or loans.

In the UK it has been widely reported that women tend to get paid less than men do in equivalent jobs and find it harder to get promoted to the same level as men with equivalent skills, qualifications and experience.

But there are now a great many men who *do* expect to

take a share in the household tasks and childcare, particularly if the woman also works. Others take on the caring role entirely and stay at home bringing up the children while the mother goes out to work, providing for the family.

However, more worryingly, according to Justice for Women there is a great inequality in the sentences given to men and women in the UK for murder of a partner. Justice for Women claim that men who kill their partners and plead diminished responsibility or provocation are more likely to walk free or get a shorter sentence for manslaughter than women who may have experienced years of violent and abusive behaviour at the hands of their male partners.

Racism and classism

The perpetrators of any racial act are aggressive whether overtly or subtly so. Men and women who are racially discriminated against may become aggressive and fight back or accept that they can no longer fight the system and become passive. Either way, their self-esteem is lowered. People who are continually discriminated against on grounds of racial prejudice will eventually lose faith in their host country and the people who run it.

People are often discriminated against because of their class too, with similar effects on self-esteem – this is especially seen in Hinduism (see *Men and women in a multi-faith world* above) although their caste system is thought to have had origins in racism and the degree of darkness in skin colour, paler skin being preferred.

Sexuality around the world

Your sexuality forms a very important part of you and if those around you cannot accept that part, or if you are discriminated against or even have threat of death hanging over you, your self-esteem is likely to suffer greatly. It may also make you feel powerless to challenge authority and battle against laws and prejudice, and it can make you angry at the injustice of it all.

How the world regards and treats lesbians, gays, bisexuals and transsexuals varies enormously. Many countries, mainly in the West, have passed laws that make homosexuality legal and will even go as far as allowing a recognised civil partnership ceremony or 'same-sex marriage' – which covers bisexuals as well as homosexuals. Headway is still to be made for equal rights for adoption (usually only one of the couples is allowed to be the adoptive parent, causing problems when the relationship fails and also through not giving equal status to both 'parents') and for custody of a child from a previous heterosexual partnership. Laws are changing fast around the world and are being updated all the time.

The harshest laws against homosexuality exist in fundamentalist Muslim countries (such as Sudan, Yemen, Iran, Afghanistan and Saudi Arabia), where a person would be given the death penalty but may be tortured or raped before being killed. Other countries have laws of varying severity from imprisonment for ten years or more, or up to ten years, or corporal punishment. For up to date information on how gays, lesbians, bisexuals and transsexuals are treated in various parts of the world visit The International Lesbian and Gay Association's website.

Even in countries where homosexuality is legal, such as in the UK and the USA, it does not mean that all individuals in those countries accept homosexuality – or that it is accepted in more fundamentalist Christian religions.

Intersex

At least one in 2000 births is ambiguous enough for professionals not to be easily able to determine what sex the baby is. Society demands that there are only two sexes and so medical intervention is thought by many to be essential – and that intervention may be given at birth instead of waiting to see what sex the person feels he or she is in young adulthood.

Some intersex adults have wished that society would support a third sex – intersex – so that they are not pressurised by doctors, families and society into choosing to be male or female. Very often they are happy as themselves and would prefer to stay that way, having their own individual identities. (For more information and support see The UK Intersex Association's website.)

19

THE FUTURE: GETTING ON WITH LIVING

Our greatest glory is not in never falling, but in rising every time we fall.
Confucius (551–479 BC)

Unhappy life experiences can prevent us from living our lives the way we want to or the way we would have done if certain things had not happened. But we need to make a stand in our own minds and say, 'No more!' We deserve better, our partners and children deserve better and our friends deserve better. With their support we can change our lives and reap the rewards of an improved existence. We need to choose our existence rather than have it choose us through being passive and not reacting in a positive way to alter the course of our lives.

Although it can seem impossible to change things, we must – or put up with continuing our lives as unfulfilled as they may be now. It is obviously preferable to move on to something better and we must find the means to motivate ourselves to making that change – or get professional help to aid us.

Letting go

It is unnecessarily draining to harbour long-term grudges in an intensely emotional way. In doing so, you allow the person who has hurt you to hurt you again by continuing to interfere in your life. If you don't need to have continued contact with someone who has harmed you in some way, drop him from your life (also see *Weeding your garden* in Chapter 9). If he is a relative and you cannot do that without arousing curiosity and people demanding to know the reasons for your behaviour, or you don't wish to bring attention to what happened, you can minimize your contact with him either by avoiding him when it is easy to do so or by, perhaps, leading a busy and fulfilled life so there is little time to include him, or by moving away.

For someone you dislike and who will be around for a long time to come because she is still friends with friends of yours, you might want to let a past betrayal lie undisturbed and start afresh but with very different ground rules from the ones you had when you first met her. You could accept her presence with equanimity: glossing over in your mind the importance of her being there as she is no longer significant in your life.

By reducing her to no more than a cardboard cut-out in your mind, you can find her company easier to accept, and you will find it easier to pass pleasantries. There needn't be any more to your relationship than a shell of a friendship where you deliberately keep her at an emotional distance while outwardly behaving quite sociably towards her. There is nothing to fear from someone you do not care about and has done the damage she has done.

Consciously letting go like this, and reducing the number of people you actively harbour grudges against, can be cathartic: you are liberating yourself from a great deal of negative emotion and waste of energy. By doing this, and by telling yourself that they can't hurt you any more, you are also shrinking their importance in your life.

However, if you find, for example, that someone close to your family who can't be dropped takes every opportunity of hurting you, ask yourself why that person feels the need to behave like this. It is very likely that the person is jealous of you and your very presence hurts him. To protect himself from the hurt you are unconsciously giving him, he fights back at you with well-aimed barbs and the like.

Change the way you think about this person. Instead of fearing the next snide comment, just think that, when it comes, that person must be dreadfully unhappy to behave like that. Point out to him that what he has said to you is hurtful or unkind if you like, but still remember to pity him. Someone to be pitied cannot be taken seriously and therefore you must be insensible to all that he says: don't let him push your buttons of vulnerability.

For other, perhaps, deeper hurt, remind yourself that the injury wasn't done especially to you: you were not singled out as being so unworthy of respect and the good things in life that you were damaged deliberately. Very often you get hurt just because you are available and can be manipulated and made to accept what is meted out to you. Forgive yourself for being the one to be in the wrong place at the wrong time with a vulnerable nature, and remind yourself that what has happened to you is not because you are a lesser person. Neither has your experience made you a lesser person; you are still worthy of respect and love.

Another part of letting go is stopping a need for everyone else's approval. The only person you really need approval from is yourself. It is also good to have approval from those closest to you – but only if they themselves are reasonable in what they expect of you.

For some people, seeking approval from others is very necessary to their self-esteem because they lack their own approval and acceptance. Try to change that by reminding yourself of the qualities you have and of the wonderful things you do. Relying on other people's approval, when you don't have your own, is risky because very often, for one reason or another, you don't get it which makes you try all the harder to yield to other people's values and wishes.

Greg was brought up in the shadow of his older brother Michael. Michael excelled at everything whereas Greg floundered at whatever task he was given. Feelings of inadequacy and inferiority to his older brother were made worse when Michael began his glowing career – a path that Greg had no hope of emulating. Greg tried everything he could think of to win his parents' approval believing that they preferred Michael because of the way they talked so admiringly and lovingly about him. This meant that, for years, Greg tried to be a second-rate Michael rather than himself: indeed, he didn't really know himself as he hadn't worked out what he was capable of, only what he was not.

Only when Greg realised that he could never be Michael in their parents' eyes did he concentrate on what he wanted for himself. This release of pressure made him all the happier and, although he could not stop being jealous of Michael, he did find things that he was better at than his brother which gave Greg a little corner of life that had not been conquered and ruled by Michael. Unskilful parenting had made Greg feel inadequate, as his parents had not tried to understand life from Greg's point of view. Instead of redressing the balance between the boys, they had increased the difference between them by talking so much of Michael and so little of Greg.

Breaking the cycle

To survive bad experiences, we must break the cycle of passing on whatever hurt or emotional damage that was done to us. This means treating colleagues, friends and partners with the respect they deserve without resorting to bullying or other negative behaviour, and treating any children we may have fairly and without undue aggression.

Friends provide general support throughout our life and their friendship can outlive our parents and the life of any partner relationship. Very often we can confide things to friends that we could not contemplate telling our parents: with each new generation there is always something that the previous one would find hard to accept or would have differing views on what has happened. And confiding to parents can be hard, as we always remain their children: we never truly grow up in their eyes so they might be more censorious than our friends or they might refuse to discuss certain topics at all.

So friends need to be valued and relationships with them nurtured, so that we can give and receive mutual support and loving.

Partners are our rock in life, taking over the need for love and support from our parents: if we treat partners unfairly, and without respect, we risk losing them – or at best, losing their regard for us. Both partners have to work hard at the relationship especially in the light of so many break-ups, many of which, as research has shown, are due to the fact that, when our own parents have divorced, the taboo of doing the same is lifted and we are less likely to fight to save our own partnership.

Another difficulty with partnerships is that we use our own parents as role models in how we should behave. If we see parents solve disagreements through violence and shouting, we are likely to choose the same methods. We must remain alert to pre-programming from our own childhood and look to others to provide alternative modelling.

Children are vulnerable and impressionable, as we know from our own upbringing. We also know what damage, if any, was done to us because of the way we were brought up. So we are in the best position to stop the cycle of hurt from parents to child through the generations. Although we cannot aim to be perfect parents (as discussed in *The ideal family* at the end of Chapter 16), we can aim to do a better job than was done with us. Having children of our own is our chance to put right what was wrong in our own upbringing and break the cycle of damage.

To replace the unskilled parenting role models of our youth, we can look around us and watch other parents to see what we can learn from them. And if we watch other parents' behaviour with their children actively rather than passively, we can evaluate their skill and decide whether what we see is helpful or unhelpful: it is unlikely a parent can show positive behaviour towards his or her children all the time. Television programmes and books on effective and appropriate childcare can also give enormous help.

Forgiveness

If you feel angry that someone has failed you, such as your parents never giving you praise, consider where they learned their behaviour. Who were their role models? It was most likely their parents. What was their upbringing like? The chances are, in essence, very similar to your own, allowing for the expected changes wrought by the generation gap. Try to forgive them for not knowing any better and look ahead, not back.

Few people reach adulthood totally unscathed by scars of their own, scars of their parents or scars of the people around them and consequently often relate to others in a harmful way such as by having a short fuse on their temper, being unable to say sorry, or never being the first one to try at reconciliation. Try to recognise these weaknesses and reduce the frequency of when they get the better of you. But when they do, limit the damage by repair work afterwards such as by an apology or an explanation of why you acted as you did.

For greater self-understanding be patient and self-forgiving if you find the situation hard to handle or if you can't cope; don't try to deny or fight against your feelings, they are an important part of your character make-up and in rejecting them you are, in part, rejecting yourself. Learn to accept how you feel and be kind to yourself in times of crises. Understand why you have those feelings to understand your inner self. If the problem is too big for you to handle alone, ask your doctor to refer you to a trained counsellor or therapist. See this as a positive step in regaining control of your life. Because you are so important, it is worthwhile making this effort, no matter how emotionally painful you fear it might be.

Moving on

We are drawing to a close in this book. You might wonder, what's next? How do you incorporate what you have learned from this book? It is important that you look at where you were at the start of the book and move on to somewhere or something better. To do this, you must precisely identify what it is that your emotional pain has prevented you from doing. Then you must work out ways to achieve your preferred goals. The time for prevaricating is gone and you must now act.

There must be so much that you can do to improve your lot in your life whether it be with family, friends, at work, or in your leisure time. Prioritise what things are most important to you and start with those. The more you work at improving your life, the more you will gain. You might not like your life but most of us believe it's the only one we're going to get, so we have to make the best of things.

Remember:

- If you can't change something in one way, change it in another.
- If you can't change the thing at all, change the way you view it.
- Be imaginative in your problem-solving.
- Is what you are doing going to get you the outcome you want?
- Be the author of your life and dare to take the next step to wherever that might be.

Here's a final quote:

A journey of a thousand miles begins with a single step.
Confucius (551–479 BC)

If your emotional pain prevents you from taking these worthwhile steps, you need to seek professional help. Remember, you are worth the effort it takes to improve your life. Good luck!

INDEX